Taking Tea

Taking Tea

Favorite Recipes *from* Notable Tearooms

hm | books

hm | books

EDITOR *Lorna Reeves*

CREATIVE DIRECTOR/PHOTOGRAPHY
Mac Jamieson

ART DIRECTOR *Cailyn Haynes*

ASSOCIATE EDITOR *Betty Terry*

COPY EDITOR *Nancy Ogburn*

EDITORIAL ASSISTANT *Janece Maze*

CONTRIBUTING EDITOR *Bruce Richardson*

STYLIST *Lucy W. Herndon*

SENIOR PHOTOGRAPHERS *John O'Hagan,
Marcy Black Simpson*

PHOTOGRAPHERS *Jim Bathie,
William Dickey, Stephanie Welbourne*

FOOD STYLIST *Janet Lambert*

SENIOR DIGITAL IMAGING SPECIALIST
Delisa McDaniel

DIGITAL IMAGING SPECIALIST *Clark Densmore*

CHAIRMAN OF THE BOARD/CEO
Phyllis Hoffman DePiano

PRESIDENT/COO *Eric W. Hoffman*

PRESIDENT/CCO *Brian Hart Hoffman*

EVP/CFO *Mary P. Cummings*

EVP/OPERATIONS & MANUFACTURING
Greg Baugh

VP/DIGITAL MEDIA *Jon Adamson*

VP/EDITORIAL *Cindy Smith Cooper*

VP/INTEGRATED MARKETING *Ray Reed*

VP/ADMINISTRATION *Lynn Lee Terry*

First published in 2016 by Hoffman Media, LLC
1900 International Park Drive, Suite 50
Birmingham, Alabama 35243
hoffmanmedia.com

ISBN 978-1-940772-31-8
Printed in China

ON THE COVER: Afternoon tea at The Peabody
Memphis in Memphis, Tennessee | Photograph by
John O'Hagan **ON THIS PAGE:** The Palm Court of
The Drake Hotel in Chicago, Illinois | Photograph by
Stephanie Welbourne

Contents

Introduction

MOST TEA LOVERS can probably recall the first time they became smitten with afternoon tea. For some, it may have happened at a luxury hotel to the sweet strains of live harp music in a breathtaking setting where the food was elaborate and the tea, excellent. For others, their first memorable teatime may have occurred at a cozy tearoom whose genial owner saw to it that the welcome was warm, the tea was hot, and the food was fresh, doting on them like a favorite family member. Whatever the venue, these are special memories to treasure.

This wonderful variety of tea experiences is precisely what we celebrate in *Taking Tea: Favorite Recipes from Notable Tearooms*. Nine hotels and nine tearooms have graciously shared recipes for some of their most popular tea fare, and we, in turn, are pleased to share their stories, as well as beautiful photography that will leave you longing for a visit. The enduring venues are all highly rated and include an array of styles and locations within the contiguous United States.

The recipes featured have been tested and adapted for the home cook. Whenever possible, we have provided measurements by volume rather than weight and have downsized the yields, though many will still serve a large teatime gathering. A number of the recipes are simple to prepare. Others may encompass somewhat advanced culinary techniques that require several hours, though we believe they are certainly well worth the time and effort.

Whether this book serves as a go-to cookbook for your next tea event or as a travel guide for your next road trip, we hope it will also serve to remind you of how you fell in love with the ritual of taking tea.

CAMELLIA'S SIN TEA PARLOR
something to feel good about

Lin Jackman (pictured above right with baker Kara Bechtold, left) encourages her customers to don a hat from the many hanging in the entryway of her charming tearoom.

―――――― ⤙⤙⤙ ――――――

Camellia's Sin Tea Parlor & Gift Shoppe
36 West Pomfret Street
Carlisle, PA 17013

717-243-6292
camellias-sin.com

In 2005, Lin Jackman decided that Carlisle, Pennsylvania, needed a tearoom. Thus was born Camellia's Sin, a name that references *Camellia sinensis*, the botanical name for tea plants.

"One of the greatest things about having a tearoom here in central Pennsylvania is to introduce people to tea," says Lin. At first, people were not very receptive to a tea parlor because they imagined that the tea served would be the same as that available at the grocery store. "They had no idea that it was bulk tea, that there were different flavors, and that it tasted so good," she explains. Still, people attending bridal showers often will announce that they are not tea drinkers. Undeterred, Lin will brew two or three different types of tea for their table from the 40-plus options in the tearoom's inventory, encouraging guests to try a little. She says that 9 times out of 10 they try it, love it, and end up buying a package of tea to take home.

In a brightly trimmed brick house that dates to 1876, Camellia's Sin is paired with a gift shop that carries everything from Polish pottery to fairy finery. In fact, the mythical creatures figure prominently in the tearoom décor, both inside and out. Tiny houses, covered in bits and pieces of broken china, dot the garden, where guests can dine in enchanted surroundings when weather permits.

The tearoom isn't open to those under the age of 6 during normal hours of operation (Wednesday through Saturday), so Lin is doing more events for children of all ages on Sundays. Fairy Tea Parties are held during the summer months, the Sugar Plum Fairy Tea in December, and the Girl and Her Favorite Doll Tea Party a couple of times a year. Also, two special Father-Daughter Teas are presented annually—one in April, the other in June. "We have the United States Army War College here," Lin says. "It's really nice to see all the officers and their little girls come in. It's really sweet!"

(Recipe is on page 13.)

Her husband, Jack, an avid gardener, supplies much of the produce for the tearoom. And although Lin makes all the soups the rest of the year, Jack, who is also a gourmet cook, makes them in winter.

Kara, whom Lin calls her "right hand," does the baking, including the customer-favorite scones. "Our scones have become really, really popular," says Lin. "People buy them now like we're a bakery." At Christmas, she sells (by preorder only) Christmas Morning Baskets, which include a baker's dozen scones, a package of tea, fresh lemon curd, and Devonshire cream, all wrapped up in a pretty basket with ribbon, to be picked up a day or two before the holiday.

Choices of up to five flavors of scones often figure in the tearoom's menu, which changes monthly and is posted on the tearoom's website. Patrons will also find a variety of finger sandwiches and sweets, and the presentation is every bit as delicious as the fare. Lin is quick to emphasize that everything, even down to the puff pastry, is made from scratch, not from a box. The only exception, she adds, is, on occasion, the bread. They always have gluten-free options and, with prior notice, can whip up vegetarian substitutes. An unlimited pot of tea is included, and customers are encouraged to try a different flavor when they have finished their first selection.

Lin insists the most important thing she has done with the tearoom is "introducing people to tea. That is something we feel good about."

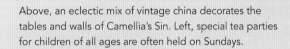

Above, an eclectic mix of vintage china decorates the tables and walls of Camellia's Sin. Left, special tea parties for children of all ages are often held on Sundays.

The
RECIPES

Courtesy of Camellia's Sin Tea Parlor

Salted Caramel–Chocolate Scones
Yield: 12

3 cups all-purpose flour
⅓ cup sugar
¼ cup instant nonfat dry milk
1 tablespoon baking powder
¾ teaspoon salt
¼ cup cold all-vegetable shortening
4 tablespoons cold salted butter, cut into pieces
1 cup semisweet chocolate morsels
1 cup caramel bits
½ cup whole buttermilk
2 large eggs
1½ teaspoons vanilla extract
1 egg white, beaten
Kosher salt

• Preheat oven to 375°.
• Line a rimmed baking sheet with parchment paper.
• In a large bowl, combine flour, sugar, instant milk, baking powder, and salt, whisking well. Using a pastry blender, cut shortening and butter into flour mixture until they resemble coarse crumbs or small peas. Add chocolate morsels and caramel bits, folding to combine. Make a well in the center of mixture.
• In another bowl, combine buttermilk, eggs, and vanilla extract, whisking well. Add to flour mixture, stirring until mixture comes together. (If dough seems dry, add more buttermilk, 1 tablespoon at a time, until dough is uniformly moist.) Working gently, bring mixture together with hands until a dough forms.
• Turn out dough onto a lightly floured surface, and shape into a large ball. Cut dough in half. Shape each piece into a ¾-inch-thick circle, pressing edges down. Brush each circle with beaten egg white, and sprinkle with kosher salt. Cut each circle into 6 wedges. Place scones 2 inches apart on prepared baking sheet.
• Bake until edges of scones are golden brown and a wooden pick inserted in the centers comes out clean, 16 to 18 minutes.

Wild Mushroom Soup
(photo on page 11)
Yield: 22 (½-cup) servings

½ cup salted butter
2 large onions, finely chopped
8 large cloves garlic, crushed
3 cups rehydrated gourmet mushroom blend, coarsely chopped
1 cup all-purpose flour
1 cup sherry or Madeira wine
6 cups chicken broth
3 cups fresh portobello mushrooms, finely chopped
1 tablespoon salt
3 cups heavy whipping cream
3 tablespoons chopped fresh thyme
Garnish: fresh thyme sprigs

• In a large stockpot, melt butter over medium-low heat. Add onions and garlic, and cook until onions are translucent, stirring occasionally. Add rehydrated mushrooms, and cook, stirring occasionally, until moisture is mostly gone.

- Add flour, and cook, stirring often, until flour looks and smells lightly toasted, 5 to 7 minutes. Add wine, and cook for 2 minutes.
- Add chicken broth, portobello mushrooms, and salt. Bring to a boil, reduce to a simmer, and cook for 15 minutes.
- Add cream and thyme, and cook for 2 minutes.
- Serve warm.
- Garnish individual servings with thyme sprigs, if desired.

Snow Fairy Cupcakes
Yield: approximately 24

1 cup unsalted butter, softened
2 cups lavender sugar*
3 cups sifted all-purpose flour
1 tablespoon baking powder
¼ teaspoon salt
1 cup water
1 tablespoon vanilla extract
5 egg whites
1 recipe Snow Fairy Icing (recipe follows)
Garnish: Wilton White Sparkling Sugar and Silver
    Metallic Hearts

- Preheat oven to 350°.
- Line 2 (12-well) muffin pans with paper liners.
- In a mixing bowl, combine butter and lavender sugar. Beat at medium-high speed with a mixer until light and fluffy.
- In another bowl, combine flour, baking powder, and salt, whisking well.
- In a liquid-measuring cup, combine water and vanilla extract.
- Add flour mixture to butter mixture in thirds, alternately with water mixture, beginning and ending with flour mixture. When all ingredients are incorporated, transfer mixture to a larger bowl.
- In a clean, dry mixing bowl, beat egg whites until stiff peaks form. Fold egg whites into flour mixture.
- Using a ¼-cup scoop, divide batter among wells of prepared pans.
- Bake until a wooden pick inserted in the centers of cupcakes comes out clean, 15 to 18 minutes. Let cool completely.
- Place Snow Fairy Icing in a pastry bag fitted with an open-star tip (Wilton #1M). Pipe icing onto cupcakes in a decorative swirl.
- Garnish cupcakes with sparkling sugar and metallic hearts, if desired.

To make lavender sugar, in the work bowl of a food processor, pulse 1 tablespoon dried lavender with 2 cups sugar until blended.

Snow Fairy Icing
Gluten-free | *Yield: 3 cups*

1 (8-ounce) package cream cheese, softened
½ cup salted butter, softened
1 tablespoon fresh lemon zest
3 tablespoons fresh lemon juice
¼ teaspoon salt
4 cups confectioners' sugar

- In a mixing bowl, combine cream cheese and butter, and beat at medium-high speed with a mixer until fluffy. Add lemon zest, lemon juice, and salt, beating to incorporate. Add confectioners' sugar, and beat at low speed until incorporated. Increase speed to high, and beat until icing is light and fluffy.

THE DRAKE HOTEL
a magnificent tradition

Extravagant décor, intimate lighting, and delightful music in The Drake Hotel's Palm Court create a lovely scene for enjoying a pot of fine tea with family and friends.

The Drake Hotel
140 E. Walton Place
at Michigan Avenue
Chicago, Illinois 60611
312-932-4619
thedrakehotel.com

The Magnificent Mile of Chicago is an iconic, metropolitan, 13-block stretch through a fast-paced city known for its stately architecture and array of cultural offerings. Along the grand mile sits one of Chicago's crown jewels: The Drake Hotel. Since the Roaring Twenties, the classic 13-story hotel and its signature rooftop sign have been a prominent feature of the city's renowned lakefront. Brothers John and Tracy Drake built the Drake, which opened on New Year's Eve 1920 to 2,000 of Chicago's most distinguished citizens. From the start, this landmark (listed on both the National Register of Historic Places and Historic Hotels of America®, the official program of the National Trust for Historic Preservation) has been touted for its refined reputation, luxurious facilities, and outstanding service. At the Drake—known as "a city within a city"—guests can expect "nothing less than The Drake Standard of Hospitality." The long list of world leaders it has hosted includes Queen Elizabeth II of England, Emperor Hirohito of Japan, Winston Churchill, Eleanor Roosevelt, Prince Charles and Princess Diana of Wales, Dwight Eisenhower, and many more.

Upon crossing the threshold of the courtyard, guests are captivated by the lavish Palm Court, situated in the center of the hotel's expansive halls, away from the frantic hustle and bustle of the busy city. A stunning crystal chandelier hangs from a mirrored ceiling and focuses on the centerpiece of the Palm Court, an exquisite antique stone urn fountain. The 275-year-old relic was acquired from New York more than 34 years ago, and the room was redecorated to complement its elaborate features that include stone cherubs and dolphins frolicking around the base of an enormous floral arrangement.

The Palm Court is a haven where Chicagoans and visitors alike come to celebrate milestones and just to savor everyday life, to enjoy life's little treasures, and to create new memories.

Countless birthday parties, bridal showers, weddings, baby showers, anniversary gatherings, community galas, and afternoon teas have unfolded within it.

Afternoon tea has been a tradition of the hotel for nearly a century. Walk-ins are welcome, but reservations are recommended. During teatime, a harpist plays from atop a flight of stairs that overlooks the court. Guests have a wide range of tea service options and are offered their choice of 17 loose-leaf selections by Palais des Thés, an all-natural premium Parisian tea brand. Each table receives a three-tiered tray layered with an array of teatime delights. Hearty English scones and diminutive quiches, all warm from the oven, grace the top tier, while sandwiches of various types, including the ever-popular cucumber, fill the next. On the final tier, mini loaves of apple or lemon-poppyseed pound cake are often served alongside elegant petits fours, delectable macarons, or tempting tartlets, such as an exotic yuzu-filled one topped with chocolate. Service options are also available to accommodate vegetarian and gluten-free diets. Tea aficionados are even invited to join the Palm Court's exclusive Loyal-Tea Club. Membership benefits include a welcome gift, complimentary afternoon tea, private member events, and more.

The Drake Hotel is well versed in the art of transporting guests to a magical place and looks forward to maintaining its magnificent afternoon-tea tradition for another 100 years.

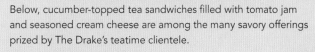

Below, cucumber-topped tea sandwiches filled with tomato jam and seasoned cream cheese are among the many savory offerings prized by The Drake's teatime clientele.

Courtesy of The Drake Hotel

Spinach–Goat Cheese Quiches
Yield: 84

1 recipe Pastry Dough for Quiche Shells (recipe follows)
1 (9-ounce) bag fresh spinach
1 (4-ounce) package goat cheese
1 cup heavy whipping cream
2 large eggs
½ teaspoon salt
¼ teaspoon ground black pepper
Garnish: crème fraîche

• Preheat oven to 350°.
• Lightly spray several mini muffin pans with cooking spray.
• Scoop 2-teaspoon portions of Pastry Dough, and press into bottom and up sides of wells of prepared pans.
• Bake for 15 minutes. Let cool in pans.
• Fill a large bowl with ice water.
• Bring a large pot of water to a boil over medium-high heat. Add spinach in batches to boiling water for 30 seconds. Remove spinach from pot, and plunge into ice water to stop cooking. Drain, and dry spinach between paper towels. Finely chop.
• Divide spinach among wells of prepared pans. Crumble goat cheese on top of spinach.
• In a large liquid-measuring cup, combine cream, eggs, salt, and pepper, whisking to blend. Divide cream mixture among prepared wells of pans.
• Bake quiches until set, 13 to 15 minutes. Let cool slightly, and remove from pans.
• Garnish each quiche with a dot of crème fraîche, if desired.

Pastry Dough for Quiche Shells
Yield: 84 (2-teaspoon) portions

3½ cups plus 1 tablespoon all-purpose flour
1½ cups potato starch
1½ cups plus 7 tablespoons salted butter
2 large eggs
½ cup water
2 tablespoons salt
2 tablespoons white distilled vinegar

• In a large bowl, combine flour and potato starch, whisking well. Using a pastry blender, cut butter into flour mixture until it resembles coarse crumbs.
• In a small bowl, combine eggs, water, and salt, whisking well. Add to flour mixture, mixing until just combined. (Do not overmix.) To prevent darkening, sprinkle vinegar over dough.
• Wrap dough in plastic wrap, and refrigerate for 2 hours before using.

The Drake Hotel Scones
Yield: 24

2½ cups plus 1 tablespoon all-purpose flour
2 cups bread flour
⅓ cup plus 1 tablespoon sugar
3 tablespoons baking powder
1 teaspoon salt
9 tablespoons cold unsalted butter, cut into pieces
1½ cups whole buttermilk
3 large eggs, divided
2 tablespoons unsalted butter, melted

• In a large bowl, combine all-purpose flour, bread flour, sugar, baking powder, and salt, whisking well. Using a pastry blender, cut butter into flour mixture until it resembles coarse crumbs.
• In a large liquid-measuring cup, combine buttermilk and 2 eggs, whisking to blend. Add to flour mixture, stirring until just combined. Bring mixture together with hands until a dough forms.
• Turn out dough onto a floured surface. Knead 4 to 5 times. Using a rolling pin, roll out dough to a ½-inch thickness. Using a 2¼-inch round cutter, cut 24 scones from dough. Place scones 2 inches apart on prepared baking sheets. Let scones rest at room temperature for 1 hour. (This is a very important step. Do not be tempted to skip it!)
• Preheat oven to 400°.
• Line 2 rimmed baking sheets with parchment paper.
• In a small bowl, beat remaining egg. Brush tops of scones with beaten egg.
• Bake until scones are light brown, approximately 10 minutes. Brush hot scones with melted butter.

Clotted Cream
Gluten-free | *Yield: 2¼ cups*

1 cup mascarpone cheese
1 tablespoon sugar
1 cup whipping cream
¼ teaspoon vanilla extract

• In the bowl of a stand mixer fitted with a whisk attachment, combine mascarpone cheese and sugar, and beat at medium-high speed until smooth. Add cream and vanilla extract, and beat at medium-high speed until thickened.
• Refrigerate until needed, up to 2 days.

Apple Pound Cakes
Yield: 15

2 teaspoons unsalted butter
1¼ cups diced peeled apples
1 cup plus 2 tablespoons unsalted butter, softened
¾ cup plus 3 tablespoons granulated sugar, divided
1 tablespoon vanilla extract
1 teaspoon salt
5 large egg yolks, lightly beaten
⅓ cup turbinado sugar (raw sugar)
5 large egg whites
1¾ cups all-purpose flour
½ teaspoon baking powder

• Preheat oven to 350°.
• Spray 15 wells of a muffin pan or mini loaf pans with baking spray with flour.
• In a skillet, heat 2 teaspoons butter over medium heat. Add apples, and cook until tender, approximately 5 minutes. Let cool.
• In the bowl of a stand mixer fitted with a paddle attachment, combine softened butter, ½ cup plus 3 tablespoons granulated sugar, vanilla extract, and salt. Beat at high speed until light and creamy.
• In another mixing bowl, combine egg yolks and turbinado sugar, beating at high speed with a whisk attachment. Add to butter mixture, folding gently to incorporate.
• In a third mixing bowl, beat egg whites and remaining ¼ cup sugar at high speed with a whisk attachment until stiff peaks form. Add to butter mixture, folding gently to combine. Add cooled apples, folding to incorporate.
• In a large bowl, combine flour and baking powder, whisking well. Add to batter, folding gently to combine. Using a ¼-cup scoop, portion batter into prepared wells of pan.
• Bake pound cakes until light golden brown, approximately 15 minutes. Let cool in pan for 10 minutes. Transfer to a wire rack, and let cool completely.

Coconut Macarons
Gluten-free | *Yield: 80 sandwich cookies*

500 grams (5 cups plus 2 tablespoons) almond flour
500 grams (4⅓ cups plus 2 tablespoons) confectioners' sugar
380 grams (approximately 11) egg whites, divided
450 grams (1¾ cups plus 4 teaspoons) granulated sugar
130 grams (⅔ cup) water
⅓ cup finely shredded unsweetened coconut
1 recipe Coconut Ganache Filling (recipe follows)

• In the work bowl of a food processor, combine almond flour and confectioners' sugar. Pulse until mixture is blended. Sift through a fine-mesh sieve.
• Add 180 grams (5) egg whites to almond mixture, stirring to form a paste.
• In a saucepan, combine granulated sugar and water. Cook until mixture registers 240° (soft-ball stage) on an instant-read or candy thermometer.
• When sugar begins to boil (212°), in a bowl, begin beating remaining 200 grams (6) egg whites at high speed with a mixer. When sugar syrup reaches soft-ball stage, gradually add to eggs whites, and continue beating until stiff peaks form.
• Add half of egg-white mixture to almond paste, folding to incorporate. Make sure first half of egg-white mixture is well incorporated before folding in second half of egg whites. Continue to fold mixture until a slow steady stream of batter falls from spatula.
• Preheat oven to 275°.
• Line several rimmed baking sheets with parchment paper or silicone baking mats.
• Transfer batter to a pastry bag fitted with a medium round tip. Pipe batter in 1-inch disks onto prepared baking sheets. Sprinkle disks with coconut. Let stand until a skin forms on macaron shells, approximately 45 minutes. (Shells should be dry to the touch.)
• Bake macarons for 18 minutes. (To test for doneness, gently wiggle macaron shells. If they wiggle with your finger, continue to bake for 1 to 2 minutes. If they have very little give, they are done.)
• Let macaron shells cool before removing from pans. Pair up macarons of equal size for filling.
• Place Coconut Ganache Filling in a pastry bag fitted with a round or star tip. Pipe filling onto one-half of each macaron pair, and top with remaining half.

Editor's Note: For consistent results, we recommend weighing macaron ingredients instead of using volume measurements.

Coconut Ganache Filling
Gluten-free | *Yield: 5 cups*

1 (14-ounce) bag sweetened shredded coconut
18 ounces white chocolate, chopped
1⅛ cups coconut milk
⅓ cup heavy whipping cream

• Place coconut in the work bowl of a food processor, and pulse until chopped.
• Place white chocolate in a heatproof bowl.
• In a saucepan, combine coconut milk and cream, and bring to a boil. Add to white chocolate, stirring until chocolate melts. Add coconut, stirring to blend.
• Let cool slightly before using.

THE ENGLISH ROSE
a place for making memories

Sharon Gilley (above left), who purchased The English Rose in 2008, says she is fortunate to have inherited Dee Grier (above right) from the tearoom's original staff.

The English Rose
1401 Market Street
Chattanooga, TN 37402
423-265-5900
englishrosetearoom.net

Sharon Gilley has a different perspective on tearooms than do many who own them. "Tearooms offer us the opportunity to step out of the ordinary and into the extraordinary for a few hours," says the proprietor of The English Rose in Chattanooga, Tennessee. "They are unique places."

In 2000, when she moved back to Chattanooga, the city where she grew up, Sharon discovered The English Rose, a local tearoom run by Angela Becksvoort, a native of the British colony of Rhodesia (now Zimbabwe). The English Rose specialized in the British style of tea, a perfect fit for Sharon, who loved this ritual. She became a regular customer. Then one day in 2010, a chance conversation with Angela changed her life. She learned that Angela was planning to retire and was interested in selling the tearoom. For Sharon, it was the perfect time to make her dreams of owning a tearoom come true.

The English Rose sits on a bustling corner of downtown Chattanooga, just across the street from the city's former train station, now a hotel. (In a strange twist of fate, the lobby of the former Grand Hotel, which sat across from the train station, now houses the tearoom.) Stepping into The English Rose gives a sense of stepping back in time. Large windows afford a view of both Market and 14th Streets, and the original penny tiles that covered the Grand Hotel lobby are on the floor. Tables of different sizes—from a private table for two to a square-top style that can seat eight people—are scattered throughout the room.

"The English Rose is a tearoom, but we have a strong lunch crowd," Sharon points out. A British-style lunch—including cottage pie, bangers and mash, and steak and mushroom pie topped with a flaky pastry—makes up the menu. For those who order afternoon tea, more delights await. Tiered stands arrive filled with warm scones, tiny tea sandwiches, and tempting desserts.

Whether lunch or afternoon tea, your meal is accompanied by a steaming pot of tea, brewed by the friendly staff. Try one of the special blends Sharon makes herself, such as English Rose Garden (a blend of black tea, citrus, roses, and hibiscus) or Lady Grantham (Earl Grey blended with lavender and a creamy vanilla finish), a tribute to the inimitable character Dame Maggie Smith played in the PBS television series *Downton Abbey*. Both teas started out as blends for a special occasion, but they have quickly become regular offerings on The English Rose's tea menu.

"The English Rose has a rich and wonderful history," Sharon says, and she considers preserving it to be part of her job. One of the joys of owning the tearoom is hearing all her customers' stories. "Over 19 years, we have had people who came here as children for their first tea experience, and now they are having baby showers," Sharon says. "People tell me how meaningful the tearoom has been in their lives. It's a joy and privilege to be a part of something that makes that kind of memories."

Housed in the lobby of Chattanooga's former Grand Hotel, The English Rose Tea Room reflects the charm of an authentic British tearoom and is suitable for all ages.

(Recipe is on page 29.)

Courtesy of The English Rose

Gluten-free Cherry and White Chocolate Scones
Yield: 10 to 12

1¾ cups gluten-free all-purpose flour blend
⅓ cup sugar
2 teaspoons baking powder
½ teaspoon salt
½ teaspoon xanthan gum
½ cup cold unsalted butter, cut into pieces
⅓ cup dried cherries, coarsely chopped
¼ cup white chocolate morsels,
    coarsely chopped
2 large eggs
⅓ cup whole milk
1 teaspoon vanilla extract
Garnish: confectioners' sugar

• Preheat oven to 400°.
• Lightly spray a rimmed baking sheet with cooking spray.
• In a large bowl, combine gluten-free flour, sugar, baking powder, salt, and xanthan gum, whisking well. Using a pastry blender, cut butter into flour mixture until it resembles coarse crumbs. Add dried cherries and white chocolate morsels, stirring to combine.
• In a separate bowl, whisk eggs until fluffy. Add milk and vanilla extract, whisking to blend. Add egg mixture to flour mixture, stirring until it is evenly moist. (If mixture seems dry, add more cream, 1 tablespoon at a time.) Bring mixture together with hands until a dough forms.
• On a gluten-free floured surface, turn out dough. Knead dough 4 to 5 turns until soft and no longer sticky. Pat dough out to a ¾-inch thickness. Using a 2½-inch round cutter, cut as many scones as possible from dough, rerolling scraps. Place scones 2 inches apart on prepared baking sheet.
• Bake until scones are light brown, 12 to 15 minutes.
• Just before serving, garnish scones with a dusting of confectioners' sugar, if desired.

Salmon Mousse Tea Sandwiches
Yield: 48

1 pound fresh salmon
¼ teaspoon salt
¼ teaspoon ground black pepper
2 tablespoons mayonnaise
1 tablespoon dried dill
2 (8-ounce) packages cream cheese, softened
2 tablespoons finely chopped red onion
2 tablespoons finely chopped celery
2 tablespoons salted butter, softened
12 slices white bread
12 slices wheat bread

• Preheat oven to 400°.
• Line a rimmed baking sheet with foil.
• Season salmon on both sides with salt and pepper.
Place on prepared baking sheet. Spread mayonnaise
on salmon, and sprinkle with dill.
• Bake until salmon is medium-well done, 15 to 20
minutes. Let cool, and cut into 2-inch pieces.
• In the work bowl of a food processor, combine cream
cheese, onion, celery, and salmon pieces. Pulse until
cream cheese and salmon are blended evenly.
• Cover mixture, and refrigerate to cool.
• Just before serving, spread butter onto bread slices.
Spread ¼ cup salmon mixture each onto buttered side
of white bread slices. Top each with a wheat bread
slice, buttered side down.
• Using a serrated bread knife, cut each sandwich
diagonally into quarters, creating 4 triangles.

Cream Cheese and Cucumber Tea Sandwiches
Yield: 32

1 (8-ounce) package cream cheese, softened
¼ cup mayonnaise
½ teaspoon dried dill
¼ teaspoon ground white pepper
⅛ teaspoon granulated garlic
8 slices white bread
8 slices wheat bread
1 tablespoon salted butter, softened
32 very thin slices English cucumber

• In the work bowl of a food processor, combine cream
cheese, mayonnaise, dill, pepper, and garlic. Pulse
several times until all ingredients are blended. Cover,
and refrigerate until needed.
• Just before serving, spread a thin layer of butter onto
bread slices. Spread 2 tablespoons cheese mixture onto
buttered side of white bread slices. Arrange cucumber
slices over cheese layer in a shingled fashion. Top each
with a wheat bread slice, buttered side down.
• Using a serrated bread knife, cut each sandwich
diagonally into quarters, creating 4 triangles.

Victoria Sponge Cake

(photo on page 26)
Yield: 12 servings

1 cup salted butter, softened, divided
¾ cup plus 2 tablespoons sugar
3 large eggs
1 teaspoon vanilla extract
1½ cups self-rising flour
¼ cup whole milk
⅓ cup strawberry jam
1 recipe Whipped Cream Icing (recipe follows)

• Preheat oven to 350°.
• Spray a 13x9-inch baking pan with cooking spray with flour.
• In a large bowl, combine ¾ cup butter and sugar. Beat at medium-high speed with a mixer until butter is light and creamy. Add eggs, one at a time, scraping bottom and sides of bowl after each addition. Add vanilla extract, beating to blend. Gradually add flour, alternately with milk, beating gently until well combined. Spread batter into prepared pan.
• Bake until cake starts to pull away from sides of pan, 15 to 18 minutes. Let cool in pan for approximately 5 minutes. Turn out onto a wire rack, and let cool completely.
• Transfer cake to a cutting board. Using a serrated knife, cut cake in half lengthwise.
• Spread 2 tablespoons softened butter on top of one cake piece. Spread strawberry jam over butter.
• Spread remaining 2 tablespoons softened butter onto top of remaining cake piece, and place, butter side down, on top of jam layer of other cake piece. Refrigerate until butter is set, approximately 1 hour.
• Spread Whipped Cream Icing over top and sides of cake, smoothing icing for a neat finish. Refrigerate remaining icing and cake until serving time, up to 3 days.
• Using a serrated knife, slice cake into 12 pieces.
• Transfer remaining icing to a pastry bag fitted with a star tip, and pipe icing rosettes onto sides of cake slices, if desired. Serve immediately.

Whipped Cream Icing

Gluten-free | *Yield: approximately 3 cups*

½ cup salted butter, softened
6 cups sifted confectioners' sugar, divided
2 to 3 tablespoons whole milk
1 teaspoon vanilla extract
1 cup heavy whipping cream

• In a large bowl, beat butter at medium speed with a mixer until smooth. Add 2 cups confectioners' sugar, beating well. Add 2 tablespoons milk and vanilla extract, beating at low speed to blend. Gradually add remaining 4 cups confectioners' sugar. Add enough additional milk to reach a firm spreading consistency.
• In a separate mixing bowl, beat cream at high speed with a mixer fitted with the whisk attachment until stiff peaks form and cream holds its shape well. Using a spatula, gently fold whipped cream into buttercream frosting until incorporated. (Icing will be soft, but should hold its shape.) Use immediately.

Profiteroles with Custard and Chocolate

Yield: 18 to 24

1 cup water
½ cup salted butter
1 cup all-purpose flour
4 large eggs
1 recipe Custard Filling (recipe follows)
Garnish: prepared chocolate syrup, confectioners' sugar, fresh strawberries

• Preheat oven to 425°.
• Line a rimmed baking sheet with parchment paper.
• In a saucepan, combine water and butter, and bring to a simmer over high heat. Reduce heat to medium, add flour, and stir rapidly with a wooden spoon. (Flour will absorb water quickly, and a dough will form and pull away from sides of pan.) Continue stirring and cooking dough for approximately 1 minute to eliminate some of water.
• Remove saucepan from heat, and set in a bowl of cool water for approximately 5 minutes.
• Using a hand mixer, beat dough for approximately 1 minute to release some of the heat. Add eggs, one at a time, mixing rapidly until each egg is combined into dough. (Dough will lose some of its shine and become sticky as eggs are incorporated.) Dough can be baked immediately at this point or refrigerated for up to a day until ready to use.
• Transfer dough to a piping bag fitted with a large tip (Ateco #829). Pipe dough onto prepared baking sheet in 1- to 2-tablespoon mounds. Press peaks down with a moistened finger.
• Bake for 10 minutes at 425°. Reduce heat to 350°, and bake until profiteroles are dry and lightly browned, 25 to 30 minutes.
• Let profiteroles cool on a wire rack. Poke a small hole in sides of profiteroles.
• Place Custard Filling in a pastry bag fitted with a medium round tip, and pipe into each profiterole through side holes to fill centers.
• Just before serving, dip tops of profiteroles into chocolate syrup, and dust with confectioners' sugar, if desired.
• Garnish with fresh strawberries, if desired.

Custard Filling
Gluten-free | *Yield: 2 cups*

1½ cups, plus 2 tablespoons whole
   milk, divided
⅔ cup sugar
6 large egg yolks
1 heaping tablespoon cornstarch
½ teaspoon vanilla extract

• In a saucepan, combine 1½ cups
milk and sugar, stirring constantly over
medium heat.
• In a medium bowl, whisk egg yolks.
Temper egg yolks by adding a few
tablespoons hot milk mixture. Slowly
incorporate remaining hot milk into egg
mixture. Return mixture to saucepan.
• Cook over low heat, stirring constantly,
until custard thickens, approximately
5 minutes. (It should be thick enough
to coat the back of a spoon. Do not
let mixture come to a boil.)
• In a small bowl, combine cornstarch
and remaining 2 tablespoons milk, stirring to blend. Gradually add to custard.
Cook, stirring constantly, until custard
reaches desired consistency.
• Remove from heat, let cool, and add
vanilla extract.
• Refrigerate until ready to fill profiteroles.

THE GRAND AMERICA HOTEL
a place for all

Afternoon tea in the Lobby Lounge of the illustrious Grand America Hotel features generous servings of delicious food, all made in-house and accompanied by personal-size pots of tea.

———— ·❦· ————

The Grand America Hotel
555 South Main Street
Salt Lake City, Utah
801-258-6707
grandamerica.com

Nestled on 10 acres in downtown Salt Lake City, Utah, The Grand America Hotel stands out as a luxurious, European-style landmark, with the Rocky Mountains as a backdrop. Its beautifully manicured gardens hint at the exquisite accommodations guests will find in this 775-room hotel, which opened in time to welcome visitors from around the world to the 2002 Winter Olympic Games. Many original paintings, including *Le Thé* by Henri Bouvet, make up the impressive private collection of art and antiques displayed throughout the hotel. The painting, which depicts a French family having tea, hangs near the Lobby Lounge, where the afternoon ritual has been observed almost daily since The Grand America opened.

Served to the strains of live harp or piano music, afternoon tea is an elegant affair that is open to hotel guests, locals, and visitors alike, with afternoon seatings at 1:00 and 3:30. Because seating in the Lobby Lounge is limited to 60 people at a time, reservations are highly recommended. "The ownership of the hotel wants everyone to feel welcome in this building, so we don't try to be exclusive in our pricing," explains Régis Perret, Director of Food and Beverage. Grand America's traditional Afternoon Tea, priced at just $28 for adults, begins with strawberries topped with chantilly cream. Guests may choose from a selection of loose-leaf teas and caffeine-free tisanes from Steven Smith Teamaker. Next, a tiered stand filled with warm scones and customary accompaniments, as well as an impressive array of six tea sandwiches and other savories, is presented. Flavors change regularly, but a classic cucumber offering is always included. "That's the one people seem to enjoy the most," says Executive Chef Fernando Soberanis.

The chicken salad, laced with pieces of grilled pineapple and bits of bacon, is also a customer favorite. "And all the bread is made in-house," notes the chef. Sometimes, there's even a savory black pepper French macaron topped with smoked salmon mousse and caviar. The last course, the sweets, is abundant enough (usually six to nine items) to require its own stand. Although flavors and types of pastries vary almost daily, patrons can always be sure a madeleine will be an option. For an additional $19, guests can upgrade their afternoon-tea experience with a glass of sparkling wine, as well as an impressive selection of cheeses.

At The Grand America, those with special dietary needs are easily and graciously accommodated. "Our goal is for any guest to feel welcome," says Chef Soberanis. With advance notice, he says, the menu can be customized for specific needs—gluten-free, vegan, vegetarian, or any other restrictions. "We really pride ourselves on being able to provide the whole experience for people," says Kasey Dubler, Director of Restaurant Operations.

Dubler says children feel special, too, when their tea fare arrives. The unique shapes of each of the tea sandwiches and pastries keep kids amused and well entertained during afternoon tea. Holiday events for occasions such as Easter, Halloween, and Christmas are popular with children and adults alike and usually sell out as soon as reservations open. He adds, "This is a place for the family and for the community."

While afternoon tea at The Grand America is special for adults, it is simply delightful for children. Below, their whimsical tea fare incorporates kid-friendly flavors and entertaining shapes.

The
RECIPES

Courtesy of The Grand America Hotel

Currant-Orange Scones
Yield: 24

3½ cups all-purpose flour
⅓ cup plus 2½ tablespoons sugar, divided
5 teaspoons baking powder
¾ teaspoon salt
1 cup cold unsalted butter, cut into pieces
½ cup dried currants
1 large orange, zested
½ cup whole milk
1 large egg
1 tablespoon heavy whipping cream

• Preheat oven to 400°.
• Line 2 rimmed baking sheets with parchment paper.
• In a large bowl, combine flour, ⅓ cup plus 1½ tablespoons sugar, baking powder, and salt, whisking well. Using a pastry blender, cut butter into flour mixture until it resembles coarse crumbs. Add currants and orange zest, stirring to combine.
• In a liquid-measuring cup, combine milk and egg, whisking well. Add to flour mixture, stirring until mixture is evenly moist. (If dough seems dry, add more milk, 1 tablespoon at a time.) Working gently, bring mixture together with hands until a dough forms.
• On a lightly floured surface, roll out dough to a 1-inch thickness. Using a 2-inch round cutter, cut 24 scones from dough, rerolling scraps as necessary. Place scones 2 inches apart on prepared baking sheets.
• Brush tops of scones with cream, and sprinkle with remaining 1 tablespoon sugar.
• Bake until scones are lightly golden, 10 to 15 minutes.

Bacon-Pineapple Chicken Salad Canapés
Yield: 28

2½ cups chopped cooked chicken breast
½ piece grilled fresh pineapple, chopped
½ cup matchstick carrots
⅓ cup sliced almonds, toasted
¼ cup finely chopped green onion
⅓ cup light mayonnaise
¼ cup plain Greek yogurt
1 tablespoon Worcestershire sauce
¼ teaspoon garlic powder
¼ teaspoon kosher salt
¼ teaspoon ground black pepper
28 mini loaves brioche or pain de sel
4 slices bacon, cooked and crumbled

• In a large bowl, combine chicken, pineapple, carrots, almonds, and green onion, tossing well.
• In a medium bowl, combine mayonnaise, yogurt, Worcestershire sauce, garlic powder, salt, and pepper, whisking to blend. Add to chicken mixture, stirring gently.
• Cut an opening or a cavity in tops of mini loaves. Divide chicken salad among loaves.
• Top chicken salad with bacon.
• Serve immediately.

Grand America Madeleines
Yield: 48

4 large eggs
½ cup plus 2 tablespoons sugar
1⅓ cups all-purpose flour
¾ teaspoon baking soda
6 tablespoons browned butter*
4½ tablespoons unsalted butter, melted
1 teaspoon fresh orange zest
1 teaspoon fresh lemon zest
1 teaspoon fresh lime zest

• Preheat oven to 350°.
• Lightly spray 4 (12-well) large madeleine pans with baking spray with flour.
• In a large bowl, combine eggs and sugar. Beat at high speed with a mixer fitted with a whisk attachment until batter reaches the ribbon stage. (When beater is lifted, batter will fall slowly in ribbonlike strands.)
• In a separate bowl, combine flour and baking soda, whisking well. Add to egg mixture alternately with butters, folding gently to combine. Add zests, folding gently until incorporated. (Be careful not to overwork batter.)
• Spoon batter into prepared madeleine pans, filling wells no more than halfway.

• Bake until madeleines are golden brown, 8 to 12 minutes. Remove from pans, and let cool completely on wire racks.

*To make browned butter, in a medium saucepan, melt butter over medium heat. Cook until butter turns a medium-brown color and has a nutty aroma, approximately 10 minutes. Remove from heat, and let cool slightly.

Editor's Note: For featherlight strands of zest, grate citrus peel with a Microplane grater.

HEIRLOOMS
A TEA ROOM FOR SPECIAL OCCASIONS
divinely inspired

Afternoon tea in a historic setting offers guests a chance to savor time-honored traditions while celebrating life's special moments with carefully selected teas and delicious, beautiful fare.

Heirlooms—A Tea Room
for Special Occasions
325 Hassan Street SE
Hutchinson, Minnesota
320-587-3975
heirloomstea.com

The adage "Silence is golden" rings especially true for Audrey Hollatz, proprietress of Heirlooms in Hutchinson, Minnesota. "God inspired the tearoom at a silent retreat I go to every year," she says.

Even from a young age, she had always loved vintage linens and having tea parties. When her own daughter was little, Audrey dreamed of having a tearoom, but the busyness of being a wife, mother, and fulltime interior designer caused those aspirations to go dormant. That is, until she went to the retreat. "I was definitely *com*pelled to do it," she says, "but it was as if I was *pro*pelled here, too."

Although Audrey hails from the suburbs of the Twin Cities, she had never heard of Hutchinson—a town an hour west that is home to Ridgewater College—until her son became interested in attending there. She recalls that on their first visit, "something in my heart went 'ping!' It was like my eyes were open to the beauty of this town, but I didn't know then how God was moving." So when the inspiration for the tearoom came later, Audrey knew that Hutchinson would be home to it. And confirmation came quickly with help from the mayor and other city officials in getting the necessary permits for this unique venue.

"We're not on Main Street and open all the time like a cafe," explains Audrey. "We're located in a historic home in a residential area, and host private events by reservation only and then our monthly CommuniTea." An elaborate, three-course afternoon affair, a CommuniTea offers smaller groups an opportunity to have tea at Heirlooms. "I have eight or nine tables, depending on how I arrange the room," she says. "This provides flexible seating options so groups can each have a private table." Each month, there is a different theme, which

necessitates changes in the décor, as well as the menu. Guests can be sure there will always be a cucumber offering, as well as a chicken salad. The flavor of the third tea sandwich, as well as those of the three sweets, changes to reflect the season. "I always do a cream scone and then a flavored scone," she explains. (Monthly CommuniTea themes are listed at *heirloomstea.com*.) Because Audrey makes all the food in-house, with advance notice, she is able to accommodate special dietary needs. "It's important, because you want people to enjoy their time here."

She also takes great pleasure in selecting three teas for each event that pair well with the fare she is serving. "Just like choosing food and wine, I'm choosing food and tea." These pairings have served as excellent ways to introduce people to different teas they might not otherwise have reason to try.

"I have met so many incredible, wonderful people through this adventure," says Audrey, whose own family has been extremely helpful and supportive of her tearoom calling. "I just thought, 'I'll have a tea party every week. Won't that be fun?'" She says that life is fuller and richer than what she could have dreamed and quotes Ephesians 4:20: "Now to Him who is able to do immeasurably more than all we ask or imagine."

(Recipe is on page 41.)

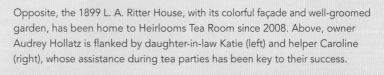

Opposite, the 1899 L. A. Ritter House, with its colorful façade and well-groomed garden, has been home to Heirlooms Tea Room since 2008. Above, owner Audrey Hollatz is flanked by daughter-in-law Katie (left) and helper Caroline (right), whose assistance during tea parties has been key to their success.

Courtesy of Heirlooms Tea Room

1¼ cups plus 1 tablespoon cold heavy whipping
   cream, divided
2 teaspoons rose water
½ teaspoon vanilla extract

• Preheat oven to 425°.
• Line a rimmed baking sheet with parchment paper.
• In a large bowl, combine flour, ¼ cup sugar, baking
powder, and salt, whisking well. Add rose petals, and
gently toss to coat with flour mixture. Make a well in
the center of flour mixture.
• In a small bowl, combine 1¼ cups cream, rose water,
and vanilla extract. Add to well in flour mixture. Gently
stir in a lifting motion until just combined, being careful
not to overmix. Add a little more cream, if needed, to
make the dough stick together.
• On a lightly floured surface, turn out dough. Knead
lightly 5 to 7 times, being careful not overwork dough.
Pat or roll dough to a 1-inch thickness. Using a 2-inch
round cutter, cut as many scones as possible from
dough, rerolling scraps as necessary. Place scones
2 inches apart on prepared baking sheet.
• Brush tops of scones with remaining 1 tablespoon
cream, and sprinkle with remaining 1 tablespoon sugar.
• Bake until scones are just lightly golden brown, 8 to
10 minutes. Transfer scones to a wire rack, and let cool
slightly before serving.

*Available from Gourmet Sweet Botanicals,
800-931-7530, gourmetsweetbotanicals.com.*

Creamy Chicken Salad in Cucumber Cups

(photo on page 40)
Gluten-free | *Yield: 16 to 18 servings*

3 English cucumbers
¼ cup plain yogurt
¼ cup sour cream
2 tablespoons chopped fresh dill
2 cups finely shredded chicken breast from
   a rotisserie chicken
1 green onion, sliced
Salt
Ground black pepper
Garnish: fresh dill sprigs

Rose Petal Cream Scones

Yield: 12 to 16

2 cups all-purpose flour
¼ cup plus 1 tablespoon sugar, divided
1 tablespoon baking powder
½ teaspoon salt
¼ cup pesticide-free rose petals*

• To prepare cucumber cups, wash cucumbers completely. Using a vegetable peeler, peel strips of skin away. Cut cucumber into 1½-inch sections. Using a spoon or mini melon baller, scoop out approximately half of center of each cucumber section. Let cucumber pieces drain in a colander, and reserve for chicken salad. Drain cucumber cups upside down on paper towels.
• Finely dice reserved cucumber pieces. (You should have approximately ½ cup.)
• In a large bowl, combine yogurt, sour cream, and dill, stirring to blend. Add chicken, green onion, and diced cucumber, stirring gently to combine. Cover, and refrigerate chicken salad until ready to serve.
• Just before serving, season cucumber cups with salt and pepper. Divide chicken salad among cucumber cups. Garnish each cup with a dill sprig, if desired.

Lavender-Lemon Bars
Yield: approximately 40

2 cups plus 3 tablespoons all-purpose flour, divided
⅔ cup confectioners' sugar
¼ cup cornstarch
2 teaspoons lavender flowers, divided
½ teaspoon plus ⅛ teaspoon salt, divided
1 cup cold unsalted butter, cut into 1-inch pieces
4 large eggs
1⅓ cups granulated sugar
⅓ cup whole milk
2 teaspoons finely grated fresh lemon zest
   (approximately 2 large lemons)
⅔ cup fresh lemon juice (3 to 4 large lemons)
Garnish: edible flowers, such as pansies or violas*

• Line a 13x9-inch baking pan with aluminum foil or parchment paper, letting edges hang over sides. Spray lightly with cooking spray.
• In a large bowl, combine 2 cups flour, confectioners' sugar, cornstarch, 1 teaspoon lavender, and ½ teaspoon salt, whisking well. Using a pastry blender, cut butter into flour mixture until it resembles coarse meal.
• Reserve 1 cup flour mixture for topping. Press remaining flour mixture firmly into bottom and approximately ½ inch up sides of prepared baking pan. Refrigerate for 20 to 30 minutes.
• While crust is chilling, preheat oven to 350°.
• Bake crust until golden brown, 20 to 30 minutes.
• In a medium bowl, combine eggs, granulated sugar, remaining 3 tablespoons flour, and remaining ⅛ teaspoon salt, whisking to blend. Add milk, lemon zest, and lemon juice, stirring to blend. Pour filling over warm crust. (It is very important that crust be warm!)
• Sprinkle reserved flour mixture over filling.

• Bake until filling feels slightly firm to the touch and topping is lightly golden, approximately 20 minutes. Let cool in pan for at least 2 hours to set.
• Using foil or parchment paper overhang, lift from pan, and place on a cutting board. If desired, trim and discard edges. Cut into small (approximately 1½-inch) squares.
• Sprinkle bars with remaining 1 teaspoon lavender buds before serving.
• Garnish each bar with an edible flower, if desired.

Edible flowers are available from Gourmet Sweet Botanicals, 800-931-7530, gourmetsweetbotanicals.com.

Expert Tip: *For best presentation, Audrey Hollatz recommends pressing straight down with the knife to cut the bars instead of using a sawing motion, and wiping the knife clean between cuts by dipping it into hot water and drying it with a clean paper towel.*

LADY BEDFORD'S TEA PARLOUR
a dream realized

Marian Caso fulfilled a life-long dream when she opened Lady Bedford's Tea Parlour in Pinehurst, North Carolina.

Lady Bedford's Tea Parlour
21 Chinquapin Road
Pinehurst, NC 28374
910-255-0100
ladybedfords.com

In naming her tearoom in Pinehurst, North Carolina, Marian Caso was inspired by the story of Anna Maria Stanhope Russell, the seventh Duchess of Bedford. Lady Bedford, a lady-in-waiting to Queen Victoria during the 1840s, is credited with inventing the British custom of afternoon tea. She experienced "a sinking feeling" every afternoon between luncheon and dinner, so Lady Bedford asked her maid to bring her a cup of tea and a light snack around 4 o'clock. Soon she began inviting friends to join her, and other people adopted the habit. By the end of Queen Victoria's 63-year reign, afternoon tea had become a British institution. Marian thought Lady Bedford's Tea Parlour was the perfect name for her tearoom, which opened in 2008.

Eight years later, Marian's charming tearoom in the heart of the Village of Pinehurst is on its way to becoming an institution in this North Carolina town. It's a favorite with locals and tourists alike. "Having tea at Lady Bedford's is like going to a spa, a lovely respite from the world," says one customer.

Marian was just 11 years old when she fell in love with the ritual of afternoon tea. Her great-aunt Helen Martyn treated her and her sister to the experience at Marshall Field's in Chicago. Marian thought the experience was "the coolest thing ever," and her love of tea was born.

Forty years passed before Marian realized her dream to open her own tearoom. She and her husband, Bill, an avid golfer, had retired to the Sandhills of North Carolina, often called "The Golf Capital of the United States." They settled in Pinehurst, where there are more than 40 golf courses within a 10-mile radius. However, Marian quickly discovered the historic village lacked one thing—a tearoom.

(Recipes are on page 47 & 48.)

"I thought, 'How can this cute, quaint little town not have a tearoom?'" Marian recalls. "It was the perfect place for one." So Marian set out to learn everything she could about opening a tearoom.

"People think it would be fun to own a tearoom," Marian says, "I thought that also." She quickly realized that she would actually be opening a restaurant. Since Marian had no previous restaurant experience, she knew she would need help—in the front of the house and in the kitchen.

To greet and serve her customers, Marian hired two friends she had met in a Bible study class, twin sisters Anne Cornell and Joan Fifield. "People love them," she points out. "They're so friendly and kind to people, and they remember everybody's name."

To handle the kitchen responsibilities, Marian turned to Anrika Colbourne, a talented pastry chef and graduate of Johnson & Wales. Her delicious sweets and pastries are equally at home on a tea tray or as the perfect finish to a lunch that begins with customer favorites, such as Kentucky Bourbon Bacon Quiche or the Anna Maria—a turkey sandwich on a croissant with cream cheese and jam—so called after the tearoom's namesake. Served with a steaming pot of one of Lady Bedford's 60-plus branded teas, how can anyone go wrong?

"We're one of the best tearooms in North Carolina according to *teamap.com*," Marian notes. "And we're frequently ranked among the top three restaurants in Pinehurst, according to Trip Advisor." Surely Lady Bedford would be proud.

Above left, twin sisters Anne Cornell and Joan Fifield greet guests at Lady Bedford's Tea Parlour. Below, the tearoom sells its own brand of teas.

The
RECIPES

Courtesy of Lady Bedford's Tea Parlour

approximately 2 inches apart on prepared baking sheet.
• In a small bowl, lightly beat egg white. Brush scones with egg white.
• Garnish tops of scones with a sprinkle of turbinado sugar, if desired.
• Bake until lightly browned, 15 to 18 minutes.

Chocolate-Strawberry Tea is available from Lady Bedford's Tea Parlour & Gift Shoppe, 910-255-0100. Any tea may be substituted in the recipe. To prepare, pour ¾ cup boiling water over 1 teaspoon dried tea leaves, and steep for 5 to 7 minutes. Strain, and discard solids.

Goat Cheese and Sun-Dried Tomato Biscuits
(photo on page 45)
Yield: 8

2¼ cups all-purpose flour
1 tablespoon baking powder
1 tablespoon sugar
¼ teaspoon salt
10 tablespoons cold unsalted butter
3 ounces goat cheese, crumbled
3 ounces sun-dried tomatoes, chopped
3 ounces whole milk
3 ounces whole buttermilk

• Preheat oven to 375°.
• Line a rimmed baking sheet with parchment paper.
• In a large bowl, combine flour, baking powder, sugar, and salt, whisking well.
• Using a coarse grater, grate butter into flour mixture. Using fingers, rub butter into flour mixture to blend. (Most of butter should be large, flat shards.)
• Add goat cheese and sun-dried tomatoes, stirring to blend.
• Add milk and buttermilk, and mix by hand or at the lowest speed of a mixer until just incorporated. (Some dry flour will remain unincorporated at the bottom of bowl.)
• On a lightly floured surface, turn out dough, and gently knead until dough just comes together, being careful not to overmix. Pat or roll out dough to a 1-inch thickness. Fold one side toward the center, and pat down. Rotate dough 90°. Repeat for three remaining sides, rotating

Chocolate-Strawberry Tea Scones
Yield: 12

3¼ cups all-purpose flour
½ cup sugar
1 tablespoon baking powder
¼ teaspoon salt
½ cup cold unsalted butter, cut into pieces
⅓ cup cold heavy whipping cream
⅓ cup prepared Chocolate-Strawberry tea*, cooled
1 large egg
1 large egg, separated
Garnish: turbinado sugar

• Preheat oven to 375°.
• Line a baking sheet with parchment paper.
• In a large bowl, combine flour, sugar, baking powder, and salt, whisking well. Using a pastry blender, cut butter into flour mixture until it resembles coarse crumbs.
• In a medium bowl, combine cream, prepared tea, egg, and egg yolk, whisking to blend. Add to flour mixture, stirring until mixture is evenly moist. (If mixture seems dry, add more cream, 1 tablespoon at a time.) Bring mixture together with hands until a dough forms.
• On a lightly floured surface, gently knead dough until smooth. Using a rolling pin, roll dough to a ¾- to 1-inch thickness. Using a 2½-inch round cutter, cut 12 scones from dough, rerolling scraps as necessary. Place scones

dough after each fold. Using a rolling pin, roll dough to a 1-inch thickness. Using a 3-inch round cutter, cut 8 biscuits from dough, rerolling scraps as necessary.
- Place biscuits on prepared baking sheet. Space 1 inch apart for flaky, crusty biscuits or ½ inch apart for softer biscuits. Let biscuits rest for 20 to 30 minutes.
- Preheat oven to 350°.
- Bake until lightly browned, approximately 20 minutes.

Kentucky Bourbon Bacon and Cheddar Quiche
(photo on page 45)
Yield: 8 servings

1 (9-inch) frozen deep-dish pie shell
4 large eggs
1 cup whole milk
1 cup heavy whipping cream
⅛ teaspoon ground black pepper
20 slices Kentucky Bourbon bacon*, cooked and
  crumbled
1½ cups shredded sharp Cheddar cheese

- Preheat oven to 375°.
- Bake pie shell for 5 minutes.
- In a small bowl, combine eggs, milk, cream, and pepper, whisking to blend. Pour into baked crust.
- Sprinkle bacon and cheese over egg mixture.
- Bake until quiche filling is set and lightly browned, approximately 30 minutes.

Kentucky Bourbon–flavored bacon is available from Father's Country Hams, 877-525-4267, fatherscountry hams.com. Regular bacon may be substituted.

Cream Puffs
Yield: 24

¾ cup water
6 tablespoons salted butter, cut into pieces
2 teaspoons sugar
¼ teaspoon salt
¾ cup all-purpose flour
3 large eggs, at room temperature
1 cup heavy whipping cream
2 tablespoons confectioners' sugar
1 teaspoon vanilla extract
Garnish: additional confectioners' sugar

- Preheat oven to 400°.
- Line 2 rimmed baking sheets with silicone baking mats or parchment paper.

- In a medium saucepan, combine water, butter, sugar, and salt. Cook over medium heat until butter melts. Add flour all at once, stirring vigorously with a wooden spoon. Cook, and stir until dough pulls away from sides of pan, 1 to 2 minutes. Remove pan from heat, and let stand for 2 minutes, stirring a few times to cool dough.
- Add eggs, one at a time, stirring constantly and vigorously with a wooden spoon until each egg is well incorporated. (Dough should be smooth and shiny.) Transfer dough to a piping bag fitted with a large round tip (Ateco #809). Pipe dough onto prepared baking sheets in 1½-inch mounds, spacing 1 inch apart. Pat dough peaks down with a damp finger.
- Bake until golden brown, approximately 20 minutes. Transfer baking sheet to a wire rack. Using a skewer or the tip of a pointed knife, poke a small hole in side of each cream puff to allow steam to escape. Let cool completely.
- In a large bowl, combine cream, confectioners' sugar, and vanilla extract. Beat at high speed with a mixer fitted with the whisk attachment until cream holds its shape and forms medium peaks. Transfer whipped cream to a pastry bag fitted with a small or medium round piping tip.
- Poke a hole in the side of each cream puff (or use previous hole), and pipe whipped cream into cream puff, filling cavity.
- Garnish cream puffs with a dusting of confectioners' sugar, if desired.
- Serve immediately.

Make-Ahead Tip: Cream puffs can be made a week in advance and frozen (unfilled) in heavy-duty resealable plastic bags. Let thaw completely before filling.

O.HENRY HOTEL
southern hospitality with old-world charm

Fragrant hot tea and freshly prepared scones, savories, and sweets inspire repeat visits for afternoon tea at the O.Henry Hotel.

The O.Henry Hotel
624 Green Valley Road
Greensboro, NC 27408
800-965-8259
ohenryhotel.com

The O.Henry Hotel makes a charming impression on guests from the moment of arrival until the time of departure. The Greensboro, North Carolina, hotel, which opened in 1998, is rooted in a tradition of Southern hospitality, world-class service, and modern features. Its proprietors, Nancy and Dennis Quaintance, named the O.Henry after William Sydney Porter, Greensboro's famed native short-story writer, who published under the moniker. The couple's mission for the hotel was to "look forward and bring back the neighborhood, community-centered hotels of old." It also paid homage to the previous O.Henry Hotel, constructed in 1919 in the town's downtown area and later demolished in the 1970s. The present-day establishment is deeply influenced by the architecture and décor, as well as the courtesies, of the past with a fine balance of contemporary style and amenities. The lobby's gorgeous wood paneling, towering ceilings, picturesque décor, and courtly staff are captivating. This delightful blend of elements makes it a perfect environment to embark on a weekend getaway or enjoy afternoon-tea service.

The O.Henry has been serving tea since its opening, and its Green Valley Grill culinary and pastry staff services and develops the afternoon-tea menus and tea selections. Tea lovers may enjoy world-class afternoon-tea service in the O.Henry's social lobby between 2:00 and 5:00 p.m., Monday through Thursday, and from noon until 5:00 p.m., Friday through Sunday. With views of the lush Don Rives Cloister Garden, teatime guests sit in cozy armchairs and on plush sofas around low tables, a setting most inviting for conversation with friends or for quiet contemplation when taking tea alone. Service options include Light Afternoon Tea, the O.Henry Tea, Tea for Two, and a Child's Tea.

Each has enticing three-tiered-tray offerings that include scones paired with clotted cream and house-made lemon curd, as well as a selection of savories and sweets that are handcrafted using local ingredients and seasonal selections. Southern-inspired spicy Cheddar rounds, which are usually nestled next to the scones, add an unexpected flavor boost to the tea fare. According to the culinary team, the cucumber sandwiches, the mini ham and brie croissants, and the chocolate-and-coconut–covered lamingtons are consistent crowd pleasers.

Guests can also select tea and beverages from the hotel's premium drink menu, which features Harney and Sons tea and includes everything from Earl Grey Supreme to English Breakfast and Sencha to Rooibos Chai. The O.Henry also offers many special tea programs throughout the year, such as the Nutcracker Tea with ornament crafting, music, and dancing; a Mad Hatter Tea featuring characters from *Alice in Wonderland*, story time, and craft time; a Wizard of Oz Tea where children enjoy crafts plus a trip down the Yellow Brick Road with Dorothy and friends; and a University of North Carolina Television–sponsored *Downton Abbey* Tea complete with period actors and etiquette lessons. Pastry Chef Erin McDermott says, "You'll often find our youngest guests enjoying their first cup of tea beside our community business leaders meeting a colleague." This Greensboro landmark, replete with Old-World charm, offers an ideal setting for making lasting memories while enjoying a wonderful afternoon tea.

The O.Henry Hotel's fusion of Old-World charm, modern style, and Southern hospitality creates a pleasurable setting for cordial conversation over tea.

The RECIPES

Courtesy of the Green Valley Grill at the O.Henry Hotel

Vanilla Mini Scones
Yield: 28

4¼ cups all-purpose flour
½ cup sugar
1½ tablespoons baking powder
1 teaspoon salt
1¼ cups cold unsalted butter, cut into pieces
1¾ cups heavy whipping cream
1½ tablespoons vanilla extract

• Preheat oven to 375°.
• Line 2 rimmed baking sheets with parchment paper.
• In a large mixing bowl, combine flour, sugar, baking powder, and salt, whisking well. Add butter, and beat at low speed with a mixer fitted with the paddle attachment until butter is pea-size, being careful not to overmix.
• In a liquid-measuring cup, combine cream and vanilla extract, stirring to blend. Add to flour mixture, mixing at low speed just until mixture comes together.
• Using a 3-tablespoon scoop, drop dough 2 inches apart onto prepared baking sheets.
• Bake until scones are golden brown, approximately 14 minutes.

Spicy Cheddar Rounds
Yield: approximately 84

2 cups all-purpose flour
8 ounces shredded sharp Cheddar cheese
4 ounces crumbled blue cheese
¼ cup grated Parmigiano-Reggiano cheese
1 teaspoon salt
1 teaspoon ground red pepper
1 cup unsalted butter, softened

• Preheat oven to 350°.
• Line several rimmed baking sheets with parchment paper.
• In a large bowl, combine flour, cheeses, salt, and red pepper. Toss well to coat cheese with flour.
• Rinse work bowl and blade assembly of a food processor under hot water, and wipe dry.
• Add cheese mixture to warm work bowl, and process until mixture resembles cornmeal. Add butter, and process until smooth.

Lemon Curd
Gluten-free | *Yield: 2 cups*

8 egg yolks
1⅓ cups sugar
2 lemons, zested
¾ cup fresh lemon juice
2 pinches salt
½ cup unsalted butter

• In a heatproof bowl, combine egg yolks, sugar, lemon zest, lemon juice, and salt. Place over a saucepan of simmering water. Cook on medium heat, stirring frequently, until bubbles begin to form and curd has thickened, approximately 30 minutes.
• Add butter, and stir until melted. Transfer curd to a bowl. Cover surface of curd with plastic wrap to prevent a skin from forming. Refrigerate until cold, 4 to 6 hours, before using.

- Divide dough into 3 portions. Wrap each portion in plastic wrap, roll up, and twist ends to secure.
- Working with one portion at a time, snip off one end from roll, and drop into a pastry bag fitted with a medium star tip (Wilton #1M). Pipe 1-inch rounds onto prepared baking sheets.
- Bake until lightly browned, approximately 9 minutes. Let cool. Store in an airtight container.

Lamingtons
Yield: 80 to 96 cake pieces

5 medium eggs, separated
¾ cup granulated sugar, divided
½ teaspoon vanilla extract
½ teaspoon almond extract
1 pinch kosher salt
¾ cup all-purpose flour
2 tablespoons unsalted butter, melted and slightly cooled
1 recipe Lamington Icing (recipe follows)
6 cups sweetened shredded coconut

- Preheat oven to 350°.
- Line an 18x13-inch rimmed baking sheet with parchment paper. Spray parchment with baking spray with flour.
- In a doubler boiler or in a heatproof bowl placed over a pot of simmering water, combine egg yolks and ½ cup sugar. Cook and stir until sugar is completely dissolved. Remove from heat, and beat at medium-high speed with a mixer until mixture is pale in color and begins to thicken, approximately 4 minutes. Add vanilla extract, almond extract, and salt.
- In a separate mixing bowl, beat egg whites at high speed until soft peaks form. Add remaining ¼ cup sugar, and beat until stiff peaks form. Fold half of egg-white mixture into egg-yolk mixture, and then fold in remaining half.
- Sift flour over egg mixture, and fold in to incorporate. Drizzle melted butter into mixture, and fold in until just incorporated. Spread batter into prepared pan.
- Bake until a wooden pick inserted in the center of cake comes out clean, approximately 15 minutes, rotating pan halfway through baking time. Invert cake onto a wire rack, and let cool completely.
- Cut cake into 2-inch squares.
- Place Lamington Icing in a small deep bowl. Dip each cake piece in icing, coating all sides well. Remove from icing, and let drain briefly on a wire rack.
- In the work bowl of a food processor, pulse coconut until finely chopped.

- Transfer coconut to a shallow bowl. Roll cake pieces in coconut, coating all sides well. Let dry completely on a wire rack.
- Just before serving, cut each cake piece in half diagonally.

Lamington Icing
Gluten-free | *Yield: 2 cups*

¾ cup whole milk
1 tablespoon unsalted butter
4 cups confectioners' sugar
⅓ cup natural unsweetened cocoa powder

- In a saucepan, combine milk and butter over medium heat until butter is completely melted.
- In a large bowl, combine confectioners' sugar and cocoa powder. Add warm milk mixture, whisking until smooth. Remove from heat, and let cool before using.

PARIS IN A CUP
tea with a little french flair

"Our crème brûlée is extremely popular," says Paris In A Cup owner Cheryl Turner, whose tearoom is patterned after upscale French tea salons.

Paris In A Cup
119 S. Glassell Street
Orange, CA 92866
714-538-9411
parisinacup.com

When Cheryl Turner's grandmother took her to tea at a Los Angeles department store, it was a magical moment for the then 5-year-old girl. "They served us little tea sandwiches on date-nut bread, and I thought I was in heaven," Cheryl recalls. "I told my grandmother, 'I want to eat like this every day!'" That, she admits, was the beginning of her love for afternoon tea.

Years later, Cheryl had an opportunity to purchase an English-style tearoom in Orange, California. She and a business partner ran it successfully for almost a decade before the partner decided to retire, so they sold the business. When the new owner closed it less than a year later, people began encouraging Cheryl to open another tearoom. She had in mind, however, to do something entirely different from her first one.

Her sister, Valerie Berry, agreed to partner with her for the new venture and to serve as chef. They began researching to find out who, besides the English, does tea. "We found out that tea is huge in France," Cheryl explains. E-mail conversations with notable Parisian tearooms, such as Angelina's and Ladurée, provided the sisters plenty of inspiration and helpful information about French tea customs. Their tearoom, Paris In A Cup, opened in 2007 almost directly across the street from Cheryl's first tearoom on Glassell Street in the heart of Orange's historic Old Towne. The décor is reminiscent of that of an upscale, Parisian tea salon, complete with elegant chandeliers, gilt mirrors, ornate wrought-iron chairs, and marble-top tables.

Many of the 135 teas on the menu are imported from highly regarded companies in France, such as Nina's of Paris and Kusmi Tea. "We have 29 of our own blends that we keep in-house all the time," says Cheryl. Tea from Harney & Sons, a New York-based purveyor, is also served.

Much of Paris In A Cup's fare is also in keeping with the tearoom's theme. The signature scones are French vanilla, though other flavors are also offered seasonally. French onion soup is always on the menu, as is the customer-favorite baked potato soup. And on the desserts menu, crème brûlée and French macarons are staples.

"The one thing we did from the very beginning is to do our tea in courses as opposed to the tiered server," says Cheryl. "We said we wanted it to be formally served no matter what they were having."

But because some customers preferred to serve themselves from a tiered server and to have their food in view during their teatime, Cheryl and Valerie put together "Tea for Two." Scones, tea sandwiches, and sweets—enough to share—are presented on tiered stands decorated with iconic French motifs such as the Eiffel Tower.

When Valerie retired in 2014, she helped Cheryl find a talented chef to take her place in the kitchen alongside longtime baker Mary Lou Wilder. The new chef, Josh Backstrom, changed the menu a little, adding more lunch items.

Paris In A Cup is open Wednesday through Sunday for lunch and afternoon tea, but it has also become well known for special events, such as the Little Black Dress Tea, Meet the Author Teas, and the ever-popular Christmas and Mother's Day celebrations.

"We are blessedly busy," Cheryl shares, "and I'm grateful for that!" She is thankful for her customers—and grateful that her grandmother instilled in her a real love for tea.

"We have a lot of dog owners who want to enjoy tea at our sidewalk café and have their furry pals along," says Cheryl. "We give the dogs treats and water." Inside the tearoom, the Eiffel Tower mural, below, gives customers a sense of being in the City of Light.

(Recipe is on page 59.)

The RECIPES

Courtesy of Paris In A Cup

Cherry-Amaretto Scones
Yield: 19
(photo on page 58)

1 cup dried cherries
1 cup almond liqueur, such as Amaretto
3½ cups all-purpose flour
1 cup sugar
1½ tablespoons baking powder
1 teaspoon baking soda
½ teaspoon salt
½ cup cold unsalted butter, cut into pieces
½ cup toasted slivered almonds
¾ cup cold heavy whipping cream
2 large eggs, divided

• Preheat oven to 350°.
• Line a rimmed baking sheet with parchment paper.
• In a small bowl, soak cherries in liqueur for 20 minutes.
• In a large bowl, combine flour, sugar, baking powder, and salt, whisking well. Using a pastry blender, cut butter into flour mixture until it resembles coarse crumbs.
• Drain cherries well, and add to flour mixture, folding to combine. Add almonds, stirring to blend.
• In a liquid-measuring cup, combine cream and 1 egg, stirring to blend. Add to flour mixture, stirring until mixture is evenly moist. (If mixture seems dry, add more cream, 1 tablespoon at a time.) Bring mixture together with hands until a dough forms.
• On a lightly floured surface, pat out dough into a ½-inch-thick circle. Using a 2¾-inch heart-shaped cutter, cut 19 scones from dough, rerolling scraps as necessary. Place scones 2 inches apart on prepared baking sheet.
• In a small bowl, beat remaining 1 egg with a splash of cream to make an egg wash. Brush tops of scones with egg wash.
• Bake for 20 minutes, turning the pan once halfway through baking time.

Pumpkin Spiced Soup
Gluten-free | *Yield: approximately 21 (6-ounce) servings*

2 large sweet potatoes, peeled and diced
  (approximately 5 cups)
4 tablespoons olive oil, divided
1 teaspoon salt, divided
½ teaspoon ground black pepper, divided
1½ cups chopped yellow onion
9 cups chicken stock
1 (30-ounce) can pumpkin purée
¼ cup firmly packed brown sugar
1 tablespoon ground ginger
1 teaspoon ground cinnamon
2 cups heavy whipping cream
Garnish: 1 recipe Candied Bacon (recipe follows)

• Preheat oven to 425°.
• Line a rimmed baking sheet with foil.
• Toss sweet potatoes with 2 tablespoons olive oil, ½ teaspoon salt, and ¼ teaspoon pepper. Spread on prepared baking sheet.
• Bake until fork tender, approximatetly 25 minutes. Remove from baking sheet, and set aside.
• In a large stockpot, heat remaining 2 tablespoons olive oil over medium-high heat. Add onion, and cook, stirring often, until onion is translucent, 5 to 10 minutes.
• Add chicken stock, pumpkin, sweet potatoes, brown sugar, ginger, cinnamon, remaining ½ teaspoon salt, and remaining ¼ teaspoon pepper. Bring to a boil, reduce heat, and simmer for 20 minutes.
• Remove soup from heat, and add cream.
• Using an immersion blender, puree soup in stockpot, or puree soup in batches in a blender, adding more chicken stock, if necessary, to make the soup smooth.
• Garnish individual servings with Candied Bacon, if desired.

Candied Bacon
Gluten-free | *Yield: 1 pound*

1 (16-ounce) package bacon
½ cup firmly packed brown sugar
½ teaspoon ground black pepper

• Preheat oven to 425°.
• Line 2 rimmed baking sheets with foil.
• Place bacon slices in a single layer on prepared baking sheets. Sprinkle bacon slices evenly with brown sugar and black pepper.
• Bake until brown sugar is melted and bacon is crisp, approximately 10 minutes. Remove bacon from baking sheet immediately, and spread on paper towels to absorb grease.
• Using a large knife, finely chop bacon, or in the work bowl of a food processor, pulse bacon until coarse.

Mixed Berry Clafoutis
Yield: 8 servings

6 ounces fresh berries*
2 cups whole milk
1 lemon, zested
1 teaspoon vanilla extract
1 teaspoon almond extract
1 vanilla bean, split and seeds scraped and reserved
¾ cup plus 2 tablespoons all-purpose flour
1 teaspoon ground cinnamon
¼ teaspoon salt
3 large eggs, at room temperature
⅓ cup granulated sugar
1½ tablespoons cold salted butter, cut into small pieces
Garnish: confectioners' sugar

• Preheat oven to 450°.
• Butter and lightly flour a 9-inch deep-dish pie pan.
• Place berries in pan.

• In a medium bowl, combine milk, lemon zest, vanilla extract, almond extract, and vanilla bean seeds, stirring to blend.
• In a large bowl, combine flour, cinnamon, and salt, whisking well. Add half of milk mixture to flour mixture, stirring until smooth. Add eggs, one at a time, whisking into batter. Add remainder of milk mixture and granulated sugar, stirring until incorporated. Pour batter over berries in prepared pie pan. Dot top of batter with butter.
• Set pie pan on a rimmed baking sheet to catch any drips that may occur during baking.
• Bake until sides begin to brown and puff up and a wooden pick inserted in the center of clafoutis comes out clean, 25 to 35 minutes. (Center of cake will not rise as much as sides.)
• Remove from pan, and let cool for 20 to 30 minutes.
• Garnish with a dusting of confectioners' sugar, if desired.

Large berries should be cut in half.

Tea-Infused Raspberry Friands
Gluten-free | Yield: 12

1 cup almond meal/flour
¾ cup gluten-free all-purpose flour blend
⅓ cup confectioners' sugar
½ teaspoon baking powder
½ cup unsalted butter, melted
1 orange, zested
1 tablespoon vanilla extract
1 teaspoon almond extract
1 vanilla bean, split and seeds scraped and reserved
5 egg whites, lightly beaten
½ cup fresh raspberries, halved
2 cups water
2 cups granulated sugar
4 tea bags orange-spice tea*
1 recipe Three-Citrus Curd (recipe follows)
Garnish: Edible flowers†, additional fresh raspberries

• All ingredients (except for Three Citrus Curd and garnishes) should be at room temperature.
• Preheat oven to 350°.
• Spray a 12-well muffin pan‡ with cooking spray.
• In a large bowl, combine almond meal, gluten-free flour, confectioners' sugar, and baking powder, whisking well.
• In another bowl, combine melted butter, orange zest, vanilla extract, almond extract, and reserved vanilla bean seeds, stirring to blend.
• Add egg whites to flour mixture, folding to incorporate. Add butter mixture, folding to incorporate. (Batter will be very sticky.)
• Spoon 2 teaspoons batter into each well of prepared pan, pressing down lightly to cover bottoms of wells. Place 2 raspberry halves in each well, followed by 2 teaspoons batter. Add 2 raspberry halves to each. Divide remaining batter among wells.
• Bake until a wooden pick inserted in the centers of friands comes out clean, 15 to 20 minutes.
• While friands are baking, combine water and granulated sugar in a saucepan, and heat until sugar dissolves. Add tea bags, and steep for time specified on package. Remove tea bags, and set tea syrup aside to cool.
• When friands are done, remove from pan by inverting onto a wire rack, and let cool slightly. Spoon tea syrup over warm friands. Repeat process until syrup is gone.
• Serve with Three-Citrus Curd.
• Garnish with edible flowers and fresh raspberries, if desired.

*Orange Spice Tea is available from Paris In A Cup, 714-538-9411, parisinacup.com.

†Edible flowers are available from Gourmet Sweet Botanicals, 800-931-7530, gourmetsweetbotanicals.com.

‡We used Nordicware's 12-well Sweetheart Roses pan.

Three-Citrus Curd
Gluten-free | Yield: approximately 3 cups

8 large egg yolks
4 large eggs
1½ cups cane sugar
1 tablespoon fresh Ruby Red grapefruit zest
1 tablespoon fresh lemon zest
1 tablespoon fresh lime zest
⅓ cup fresh Ruby Red grapefruit juice
⅓ cup fresh lemon juice
⅓ cup fresh lime juice
1 pinch kosher salt
½ cup cold butter, cut into small pieces

• In a metal bowl, combine egg yolks, eggs, sugar, zests, and juices, whisking until blended. Set bowl over a saucepan partially filled with water, but do not let water touch the bowl. Cook over medium heat, stirring often, until mixture is thick enough to coat the back of a wooden spoon, approximately 5 minutes. Remove from heat.
• Add salt, then butter, a few pieces at a time, to mixture, whisking until completely combined.
• Strain curd through a fine-mesh sieve. Transfer strained curd to a bowl, and place plastic wrap directly on curd surface to keep a skin from forming. Cover with an airtight lid. Refrigerate overnight before using.*

*Curd can be refrigerated for up to a week or frozen for up to 2 months. Thaw in the refrigerator for 24 hours. Do not heat.

PARK HYATT AVIARA RESORT
a calming experience

Teatime patrons of the Park Hyatt Aviara Resort may see and smell the loose-leaf tea blends before selecting one to enjoy along with the delicious fare.

Park Hyatt Aviara Resort
7100 Aviara Resort Drive
Carlsbad, CA 92011
760-448-1234
parkaviara.hyatt.com

Tucked into the master-planned community of Aviara among an 18-hole Arnold Palmer-designed golf course sits the stunning Park Hyatt Aviara Resort. It's scenic 200-acre estate is just minutes away from the South Carlsbad State Beach and a brief 45-minute drive north of San Diego, California. The cool breeze from the Pacific Ocean is as welcoming as the staff of the resort who greet guests warmly. Constructed in a Spanish Colonial architectural style, the luxurious facility includes three remarkable dining options: an Italian restaurant, a steakhouse, and a California-style bistro with a lounge and live entertainment. There are also seven tennis courts, two outdoor pools, a day spa, and plenty of amenities for visitors with children, including a day camp, game room, and onsite babysitting services.

Soothing sounds of live piano music can be heard throughout the hallways as guests make their way to the sunny Lobby Lounge, where afternoon tea is served Friday and Saturday between 2:00 and 3:30 p.m. Since 1997, the Park Hyatt Aviara Resort has served a by-reservation-only afternoon tea. The English-style service is presented on tiered stands to patrons seated at elegant dining tables, as well as those who prefer to take tea at low tables while relaxing on clusters of cozy couches or in comfortable armchairs—all with exquisite views of Batiquitos Lagoon and of the Pacific Ocean.

Executive Chef Pierre Albaladejo presents a menu for the traditional afternoon ritual that incorporates seasonal selections but also features many tried-and-true favorites. (To ensure patrons with special dietary needs are able to enjoy their teatime, gluten-free and vegan menu options are available.) Luscious strawberry-topped yogurt–panna cotta mousse parfaits and warm made-from-scratch sultana scones, served with Devonshire cream and tangy lemon curd, are a

delightful start. Next, the savories course consists of four to five delicious tea-size options, including curried chicken salad in pastry shells, smoked salmon canapés, and sliced cucumber tea sandwiches. Fruit flavors abound in the desserts course. French macarons, chocolate-dipped strawberries, and petite fruit tarts filled with vanilla cream are among the sweets tea goers will find on the final tier, along with other flavorful creations from the resort's talented pastry chefs.

Small glass jars containing exclusive medleys of fine loose-leaf tea choices from Mighty Leaf are presented tableside in a sampler box. Selections include traditional black tea, Earl Grey Organic, and Green Tea Jasmine, as well as intriguing flavored blends such as Brazilian Fruit, Chocolate Orange Truffle, Pear Caramel, Silver Jasmine, African Amber Organic, Wild Blossoms and Berries, and Chamomile Citron. "Our customers can experience the aroma of each tea and choose their favorite," explains Chef Albaladejo. To complete their afternoon-tea experience, guests may order a glass of sparkling wine, tawny port, or dry sherry along with their tea service, if they wish.

The flavorsome beverages, delectable food, and attentive service combined with calming views of scenic waterfronts, a vivid azure sky, cascading orchids, and lush palm trees will leave tea aficionados longing for another visit to the Park Hyatt Aviara Resort.

Glimpses of bright blue sky and verdant palm trees through the lounge's large windows enchant guests as they enjoy afternoon tea.

Courtesy of Park Hyatt Aviara Resort

stirring with a fork to form a soft dough. Add raisins, stirring to combine.
• On a lightly floured surface, roll out dough to a ½-inch thickness. Using a 2-inch round cutter, cut 9 scones from dough, rerolling scraps as necessary. Place scones 2 inches apart on prepared baking sheet.
• Brush tops of scones with beaten egg.
• Bake until scones are golden, 12 to 16 minutes.

Strawberry & Vanilla Yogurt–Panna Cotta Mousse Parfaits
Gluten-free | *Yield: 24 servings*

2 cups heavy whipping cream
2 cups plain yogurt
½ cup sugar
1½ teaspoons unflavored gelatin
1 tablespoon cold water
1 tablespoon honey
1½ teaspoons vanilla extract
1 recipe Strawberry Coulis (recipe follows)
1 cup diced fresh strawberries
24 amaretto cookies
Garnish: fresh strawberry halves

• In a large mixing bowl, beat cream at high speed with a mixer fitted with a whisk attachment until medium-stiff peaks form.
• In a separate bowl, combine yogurt and sugar, whisking by hand to blend and dissolve sugar.
• In a small bowl, sprinkle gelatin over cold water. Let stand for 1 minute.
• In a small saucepan, combine honey and vanilla extract, and bring to a boil. Remove from heat, and add gelatin mixture. Return saucepan to heat until gelatin is melted.
• Add honey mixture to yogurt mixture, whisking well to incorporate. Slowly fold whipped cream into yogurt mixture. Refrigerate mousse for several hours until set.
• Place yogurt mousse in a piping bag fitted with a star tip.
• Divide Strawberry Coulis among 24 small glasses slightly larger than the diameter of an amaretto cookie. Top evenly with diced strawberries. Pipe half of mousse over strawberries in each glass. Add an amaretto cookie to each, followed by remaining mousse.
• Garnish with fresh strawberries, if desired.

Sultana Scones
Yield: 9

1½ cups all-purpose flour
1 teaspoon baking powder
1 teaspoon salt
½ teaspoon baking soda
3 tablespoons cold unsalted butter, cut into pieces
¾ cup whole buttermilk
1 teaspoon vanilla extract
⅓ cup golden raisins
1 large egg, lightly beaten

• Preheat oven to 350°.
• Line a rimmed baking sheet with parchment paper.
• In a large bowl, combine flour, baking powder, salt, and baking soda, whisking well. Using a pastry blender, cut butter into flour mixture until it resembles coarse crumbs.
• In a liquid-measuring cup, combine buttermilk and vanilla extract, stirring to blend. Add to flour mixture,

Strawberry Coulis
Gluten-free | *Yield: approximately 3 cups*

4 cups sliced fresh strawberries
¾ cup water
3 tablespoons sugar

• In a saucepan, combine strawberries, water, and sugar. Bring to a boil, reduce heat, and let simmer for 5 minutes. Let cool slightly.
• Transfer strawberry mixture to the container of a blender, and blend until smooth.
• Pass coulis through a very fine–mesh sieve to remove all seeds.
• Refrigerate until cold.

Raspberry French Macarons
Gluten-free | *Yield: approximately 42 sandwich cookies*

250 grams (2½ cups) confectioners' sugar
250 grams (2½ cups) almond flour
188 grams (approximately 6) egg whites,
  at room temperature, divided
Red food coloring
250 grams (1 cup) granulated sugar
63 grams (¼ cup) water
1 pinch (⅛ teaspoon) egg-white powder
1 recipe Raspberry Ganache Filling (recipe follows)

• In the work bowl of a food processor, combine confectioners' sugar and almond flour. Process until finely ground.
• In a large mixing bowl, combine 93 grams (3) egg whites and almond flour mixture. Beat at medium speed with a mixer until well incorporated. Add desired amount of food coloring to tint almond mixture, if desired.
• In a saucepan, combine granulated sugar and water, and cook over medium heat until mixture reaches soft-ball stage (235° to 240°).
• In a small mixing bowl, combine remaining 95 grams (3) egg whites and egg-white powder. Beat at high speed with the whisk attachment of a mixer until soft peaks form. Slowly add hot syrup to egg whites to make an Italian meringue. Beat at medium speed until meringue has thickened and cooled. (Bowl should be slightly warm to the touch.)
• Add meringue, a little at a time, to the almond mixture, beating until well mixed and batter is loose.
• Preheat oven to 270°.
• Line several rimmed baking sheets with parchment paper.

• Place batter in a piping bag fitted with a large round tip (Ateco #805). Pipe batter onto prepared baking sheets in quarter-size rounds. Let stand for 20 minutes to create a skin on the macarons.
• Bake until firm to the touch, 17 to 20 minutes. Let cool completely on baking sheets.
• Refrigerate macarons overnight before filling.
• Place Raspberry Ganache Filling in a pastry bag fitted with a medium round tip. Pipe filling onto flat surface of one macaron. Top with another macaron, flat side down. Repeat with remaining macarons and filling.

Editor's Note: For consistent results, we recommend weighing macaron ingredients instead of using volume measurements.

Raspberry Ganache Filling
Gluten-free | *Yield: 2 cups*

9 ounces white chocolate, chopped
250 grams (¾ cup plus 4 teaspoons) raspberry purée
1 cup butter, at room temperature

• Place white chocolate in a bowl.
• In a small saucepan, bring raspberry purée to a boil. Pour hot purée over white chocolate, whisking until smooth and shiny. Add butter, whisking until smooth and incorporated.
• Let ganache sit overnight to set before using.

THE PEABODY HOTEL
pageantry and tea

Whether you come to see The Peabody's famous water fowl take their twice daily bath in the lobby fountain, above, or to experience the impeccable service at Chez Philippe, afternoon tea at this landmark Memphis hotel is a memorable event.

The Peabody Memphis
149 Union Avenue
Memphis, TN 38103
901-529-4000
peabodymemphis.com

Memphis, Tennessee, stands as one of the icons in the world of ribs and pulled pork, and the tangy aroma of pit-house smoke is never far from your nose. But what's a tea lover to do between the time it takes to eat a generous lunch platter at Central BBQ and a dinner of finger-licking ribs at Rendezvous? You leave the world of smoked meats and sweet iced teas far behind and head downtown for a bit of afternoon elegance at that other great Memphis icon, The Peabody hotel.

The afternoon-tea experience at The Peabody Memphis is unlike that at any other hotel tearoom in the world because duck is always featured. No, you won't find duck on the menu. (It has been banned from the hotel's menu since 1981, making Chez Philippe quite possibly the only French restaurant in the world that does not serve duck. And duck pâté will never be served at teatime.) The ducks are on parade in the lobby.

Just as they have done for more than 75 years, at exactly 11:00 a.m. and 5:00 p.m. each day, the elevator doors open, and the Peabody ducks march down a red carpet and dive into the marble fountain in the hotel lobby. There they spend several hours swimming and splashing to the delight of hundreds of admirers who have traveled to Memphis from around the world to see this daily pageantry. These prized fowl celebrities are under the tutelage of Anthony Petrina, The Peabody's official duckmaster, who has the vocation every wide-eyed child in the audience would love to call their own.

Afternoon tea at The Peabody takes place Wednesday through Saturday from 1:00 p.m. until 3:30 p.m. in the hotel's luxurious French restaurant, Chez Philippe. This palatial setting—complete with mirrored walls and gilded accents, all lit by crystal chandeliers and sconces—is reminiscent of the settings for tea at The Ritz in London or The St. Regis in New York. Every detail has been meticulously thought out, leading diners to expect an afternoon tea that matches the caliber of the surroundings.

After tea is poured, guests watch with pleasure as the well-rehearsed teatime performance continues to unfold. Plump, warm scones with Devonshire cream and lemon curd are the first to appear. The tiered silver server then arrives laden with sandwiches featuring delicious fillings such as smoked salmon, crab salad, Roquefort-chicken salad, cantaloupe and prosciutto, and cucumber with tomato, each as appealing to the eye as to the palate.

You expect the pastries at a French restaurant to be exceptional, and Chez Philippe never disappoints, with creative masterworks such as macadamia-caramel tarts, pistachio-brandy-cherry financièrs, and hazelnut-chocolate shortbread. Thankfully, the thoughtful staff is always happy to box the leftovers.

The three-course Chez Philippe Afternoon Tea can also include an optional champagne course, and for children ages 12 and younger, a lighter Duckie Tea is offered. The resourceful chefs will gladly prepare a gluten-free tea when requested with your reservation.

Having fully enjoyed a sumptuous afternoon-tea retreat at the grand Peabody hotel, a stroll past the music joints along Beale Street is in order. After all, you'll need to revive your appetite before dinner.

Above left, children will be delighted to see The Peabody's ducks while adults enjoy the sumptuous tea trays served at Chez Philippe. Don't worry if you can't finish it all. The restaurant's servers will be glad to box the leftovers.

Courtesy of Peabody Hotel

1 cup whole milk
¼ cup plus 1 tablespoon heavy whipping cream, divided
2 large eggs, divided
1½ teaspoons vanilla extract

• Preheat oven to 400°.
• Line a baking sheet with parchment paper.
• In a large bowl, combine flour, sugar, baking powder, and salt, whisking well. Using a pastry cutter, cut butter into flour mixture until it resembles coarse crumbs. Add dried fruit, stirring to incorporate.
• In a medium bowl, combine milk, ¼ cup cream, 1 egg, and vanilla extract, stirring to blend. Add to flour mixture, stirring until just combined. (Do not overmix.)
• On a lightly floured surface and using a rolling pin, roll out dough to a ¾-inch thickness. Using a 3-inch round cutter, cut as many scones as possible from dough, rerolling scraps. Place 2 inches apart on prepared baking sheet.
• In a small bowl, combine remaining 1 egg and remaining 1 tablespoon cream, whisking well. Brush egg mixture onto tops of scones.
• Bake until scones are golden brown and a wooden pick inserted in the centers comes out clean, 15 to 18 minutes.

Roquefort–Chicken Salad Croissants
Yield: 16

2 (8-ounce) boneless skinless chicken breasts
¼ teaspoon salt
⅛ teaspoon ground black pepper
¾ cup chopped celery
2 tablespoons finely chopped shallot
1 sprig fresh rosemary, finely chopped
1 sprig fresh thyme, finely chopped
2 tablespoons fresh lemon juice
1 tablespoon finely chopped Roquefort cheese
¼ cup mayonnaise
16 mini croissants
Garnish: microgreens*

• Preheat oven to 400°.
• Line a rimmed baking sheet with aluminum foil.

Dried Fruit Scones
Yield: 10 to 12

4 cups pastry flour
¼ cup sugar
2 tablespoons plus 2 teaspoons baking powder
⅛ teaspoon salt
1 cup cold unsalted butter, cut into cubes
¾ cup dried fruit, such as dried cranberries, dried currants, or golden raisins

- Season chicken breasts with salt and pepper, and place on prepared baking sheet.
- Roast until an instant-read thermometer registers 160° when inserted into the thickest part of chicken breasts, 10 to 12 minutes. Let cool completely. Cut cooled chicken into ½-inch cubes.
- In a bowl, combine chicken, celery, shallot, rosemary, and thyme. Add lemon juice and cheese, stirring to blend. Add mayonnaise, stirring to combine. Cover, and refrigerate until just before serving time.
- Slice croissants in half lengthwise, being careful not to cut all the way through. Fill each croissant with 2 tablespoons chicken salad.
- Garnish each croissant with microgreens, if desired.
- Serve immediately.

Microgreens are available at many grocery stores. They are also available from Gourmet Sweet Botanicals, 800-931-7530, gourmetsweetbotanicals.com.

Crab Salad Canapés
Yield: 40

1 pound fresh jumbo lump crabmeat
¾ cup finely chopped celery
1 teaspoon finely chopped shallot
1 sprig fresh rosemary, finely chopped
1 sprig fresh thyme, finely chopped
1 sprig fresh parsley, finely chopped
1 lemon, zested and juiced
2 teaspoons Old Bay Seasoning
¼ cup mayonnaise
¼ teaspoon salt
¼ teaspoon ground black pepper
40 mini toasts
Garnish: mandarin orange sections

- Place crab in a large bowl, and pick over crab to remove any pieces of shell.
- In another bowl, combine celery, shallot, rosemary, thyme, and parsley, stirring to blend. Add lemon zest and juice and Old Bay Seasoning, stirring to incorporate. Add celery mixture to crab, stirring to blend. Gently fold in mayonnaise, salt, and pepper. Cover, and refrigerate until just before serving time.
- Using 2 small teaspoons, shape crab mixture into quenelles (small ovals), and place on each mini toast.
- Garnish with a mandarin orange section, if desired.
- Serve immediately.

- Prepare dipping chocolate according to package instructions. Dip cookies halfway into chocolate. Place on wire racks to allow chocolate to set.
- Garnish cookies with hazelnuts while chocolate is still soft, if desired.

Almond Financiers
Yield: 24

½ cup unsalted butter
1 teaspoon vanilla extract
1 cup confectioners' sugar
½ cup almond flour
⅓ cup all-purpose flour
1 pinch salt
3 egg whites, lightly beaten
1 recipe Raspberry Buttercream (recipe follows)
Garnish: pearlized white dragées, dark chocolate curls

- In a saucepan, melt butter over medium heat. Cook until browned and fragrant, being careful not to burn. Let cool slightly. Add vanilla extract, stirring to combine.
- Preheat oven to 350°.
- Spray a 24-well mini muffin pan with baking spray with flour.
- In a large bowl, combine confectioners' sugar, almond flour, all-purpose flour, and salt, whisking well. Add egg whites, stirring until just combined. Add cooled butter, stirring until just combined.
- Divide batter among wells of prepared pan.
- Bake until a wooden pick inserted in the centers comes out clean, 10 to 13 minutes. Invert onto a wire rack, and let cool completely.
- Place Raspberry Buttercream in a pastry bag fitted with a small star tip (Wilton #16), and pipe a swirl onto each financier.
- Garnish each financier with a dragée and a chocolate curl, if desired.

Raspberry Buttercream
Gluten-free | *Yield: 1 cup*

½ cup unsalted butter, softened
2 cups confectioners' sugar
1 pinch salt
1 tablespoon whole milk
½ teaspoon raspberry extract
Red food coloring

- In a large mixing bowl, combine butter, confectioners' sugar, salt, milk, and raspberry extract. Beat with a mixer, starting at low speed and gradually increasing to high speed, until smooth and creamy. Tint buttercream with desired amount of food coloring.

Hazelnut-Chocolate Shortbread
Yield: 72

1 cup unsalted butter, softened
1 cup sugar
1 large egg
1 teaspoon vanilla extract
2 cups all-purpose flour
¾ cup natural unsweetened cocoa powder
1½ teaspoons baking powder
1 teaspoon salt
1 (7-ounce) container semisweet dipping chocolate
Garnish: chopped glazed hazelnuts

- Preheat oven to 350°.
- Line several rimmed baking sheets with parchment paper.
- In a large mixing bowl, combine butter and sugar, beating at medium-high speed with a mixer until light and fluffy. Add egg and vanilla extract, beating to combine.
- In another bowl, combine flour, cocoa powder, baking powder, and salt, whisking well. Add flour mixture to butter mixture, beating until just combined. Wrap dough in plastic wrap, and refrigerate for 1 hour.
- On a lightly floured surface and using a rolling pin, roll dough to a ⅛-inch thickness. Using a 2-inch scalloped round cutter, cut cookies from dough. Place cookies 2 inches apart on prepared baking sheets.
- Bake for 10 to 12 minutes. Let cookies cool on baking sheets for 5 minutes before transferring to wire racks to cool completely.

QUEEN MARY TEA ROOM
a really good cup of tea

Wearing her signature tiara and royal purple dress, the queen herself, Mary Greengo, greets guests at Queen Mary Tea Room in Seattle, Washington.

—— ·‹‹‹‹‹· ——

Queen Mary Tea Room and Restaurant
2912 NE 55th Street,
Seattle, WA 98105
206-527-2770
queenmarytea.com

Tea has been part of Mary Greengo's life almost from birth. "I've probably had a cup of tea every day since I was 2 years old," says the owner of Queen Mary Tea Room in Seattle, Washington. Although Queen Mary (as she is known to her patrons and her employees) is a Seattle native, she has British great-grandparents on both sides of her family. "Drinking tea is just part of my DNA," she says.

Perhaps it's no surprise that after earning a culinary degree, as well as a baking and specialty-pastry degree, Mary decided to open a tearoom in her hometown 28 years ago. Some people thought she was crazy to start the venture in Seattle, where loose-leaf tea was an unknown commodity at the time. But Mary wanted to be her own boss.

She found the perfect name for her new business quite by accident. At the end of a lunch out with friends, Mary ordered a cup of tea. The waiter brought her an herbal tea bag and a mug of lukewarm water that tasted like coffee. So Mary did what any self-respecting tea lover would have done. She sent the tea back, exclaiming, "Egad! Can't anybody make a decent cup of tea?"

Her amused friends immediately began to tease her: "Queen Mary has to have her tea a certain way."

"I thought, 'That's it!'" Mary recalls. "'Queen Mary will be the name of my tearoom.'"

So in 1988, she opened Queen Mary Tea Room & Restaurant in the heart of Seattle's Ravenna neighborhood, just a few blocks from the University of Washington. Here, Mary insists on using only the freshest ingredients. "We make everything from scratch," she says. "Everything tastes real, and it satisfies you more."

If there is one thing Mary is more particular about than the food she serves in her restaurant, it's the tea. On any given day, more than 80 varieties of tea and tea blends are on offer.

"Before any tea makes it onto Queen Mary's shelves, we have tastings with my entire staff of 28 people," Mary explains. "There's a whole ritual to how we do it. No one is allowed to talk while we're tasting teas; everybody writes down their thoughts. We all need to buy off on each tea."

In the restaurant and at the Queen Mary Emporium, which opened just down the street in 2011, Mary's teas are marketed under her own Queen Mary brand. She comes up with the ideas for tea blends and blends them herself. "I love teas that are full-bodied, that are complex and have depth to them—well-rounded smooth teas with a lot of flavor in them," she explains. "I don't like bitter or astringent. You won't ever find that in my teas."

Every tea has its unique label with original graphics, which she designs. "These teas are my children," Mary says. "Every tea is a beauty unto itself."

Several years ago, she created another way to market her teas—a direct-selling program known as Tea Queens by Queen Mary. She helps women around the United States start their own home-based tea-party businesses, providing the training and tea knowledge they will need through videos, brochures, and web-based meetings. Her Tea Queens sell her branded teas, as well as other tea merchandise, through the parties they give, receiving a commission on their sales.

"It's a great way for women to connect with their friends through tea," Mary explains. "I started Tea Queens by Queen Mary so that women could create their own path to financial success while enjoying good company and a great cup of tea."

Above left, Mary Greengo invites her guests, who come from all over the world, to mark their hometowns with a push pin on a map. Mary personally blends the tearoom's successful line of Queen Mary teas, left.

OPEN AND DISCOVER QUEEN MARY TEAS

Courtesy of Queen Mary Tea Room

Salmon Mousse Canapés
Yield: 16 to 20

1 teaspoon olive oil
2 tablespoons chopped scallions
1 (4-ounce) package smoked salmon
1 (8-ounce) package cream cheese, softened
2 teaspoons fresh lemon juice
½ teaspoon dried dill
1 loaf multigrain bread, unsliced

• In a skillet, heat olive oil over medium-high heat. Add scallions, and sauté until wilted and soft.
• In the work bowl of a food processor, combine scallions and smoked salmon, and pulse to shred. Scrape sides of bowl, and add cream cheese, lemon juice, and dill. Process until mixture is smooth.
• Transfer salmon mixture to a covered container, and refrigerate for a few hours until needed.
• Using a large bread knife, cut bread into ¾-inch slices. Freeze bread slices until firm.
• Using a 1½-inch square cutter, cut as many shapes as possible from frozen bread slices, discarding scraps. Cover bread squares with damp paper towels, and let thaw for 15 to 30 minutes.
• Transfer salmon mixture to a pastry bag fitted with a medium star tip (Wilton #1M). Pipe rosettes of salmon mixture onto bread squares in a decorative swirl.

Chicken-Almond Tea Sandwiches
Yield: 16

1 tablespoon olive oil
2 (8-ounce) boneless skinless chicken breasts
½ teaspoon salt
¼ teaspoon ground white pepper
2 tablespoons stone-ground mustard
¼ teaspoon Mrs. Dash
2 tablespoons ground toasted almonds
½ to ¾ cup heavy whipping cream
8 slices white sandwich bread
Garnish: additional ground toasted almonds

• In a skillet, heat olive oil over medium-high heat. Add chicken breasts, and cook until opaque. Transfer chicken to a plate, and season with salt and white pepper. Let cool.

• Place cooled chicken in the work bowl of a food processor; pulse to break into smaller pieces. Add mustard, Mrs. Dash, and almonds, pulsing a few times to blend. Add ½ cup cream, and process until smooth. (If mixture seems dry, add more cream as food processor is running to reach a spreadable consistency. Be careful not to overwork or filling will be too smooth and texture will be ruined. If additional cream is needed, add and mix by hand.)
• Spread chicken mixture evenly onto 4 bread slices. Top each with another bread slice. Trim and discard crusts from sandwiches. Cut each sandwich into 4 fingers.
• Garnish cut edges of tea sandwiches with additional ground almonds, if desired.

Cucumber Salad Canapés
Gluten-free | *Yield: 36 to 40*

1 (8-ounce) package cream cheese, softened
¼ cup mayonnaise
1 tablespoon minced fresh dill
1½ teaspoons fresh lemon juice
½ teaspoon Worcestershire sauce
¼ teaspoon salt
⅛ teaspoon ground red pepper
⅛ teaspoon ground black pepper
1½ cups finely chopped and seeded
   English cucumber
½ cup finely chopped red bell pepper
¼ cup finely chopped white onion
2 tablespoons chopped fresh parsley
1 tablespoon capers, rinsed and chopped
1 English cucumber, cut into ¼-inch slices

• In a large mixing bowl, combine cream cheese, mayonnaise, dill, lemon juice, Worcestershire sauce, salt, red pepper, and black pepper. Beat at medium speed with a mixer until smooth.
• Add cucumber, red bell pepper, onion, parsley, and capers, folding to combine. Taste cucumber salad, and season with more salt and pepper, if desired.
• Gently scoop out cucumber slices, creating a shallow well. Divide cucumber salad among cucumber slices.
• Serve immediately.

Goat Cheese–Apple Tea Sandwiches
Yield: 16

1 (8-ounce) package cream cheese, softened
6 ounces goat cheese, softened
2 ounces toasted hazelnuts, ground
1 teaspoon Mrs. Dash
4 slices white bread
4 slices wheat bread
2 Fuji apples, thinly sliced

• In the work bowl of a food processor, combine cream cheese, goat cheese, hazelnuts, and Mrs. Dash. Pulse until well combined.
• Transfer cheese mixture to a covered container, and refrigerate for several hours until needed.
• Spread cheese mixture onto white bread slices. Top cheese layer with a layer of apple slices. Spread cheese mixture onto wheat bread slices. Place each, cheese layer down, on top of apple layer.
• Using a serrated bread knife, trim crusts from sandwiches, creating squares. (Discard crusts.) Cut each sandwich diagonally into quarters, creating 4 triangles.

Chocolate-Raspberry Cake
Yield: 12 servings

1½ cups all-purpose flour
¾ cup natural unsweetened cocoa powder
1½ teaspoons baking powder
¾ teaspoon baking soda
½ teaspoon salt
¾ cup unsalted butter, softened
1½ cups sugar
1½ teaspoons raspberry extract
3 large eggs
1 cup whole milk
1 recipe Chocolate-Raspberry Mousse (recipe follows)
Garnish: grated semisweet chocolate, raspberry jelly,
   fresh raspberries

• Preheat oven to 350°.
• Spray 3 (9-inch) round cake pans with baking spray
with flour.
• In a large bowl, combine flour, cocoa powder, baking
powder, baking soda, and salt, whisking well.
• In large mixing bowl, combine butter, sugar, and
raspberry extract, beating at medium-high speed with
a mixer until light and fluffy, 3 to 5 minutes. Add eggs,
one at a time, beating well after each addition.
• Add flour mixture to butter mixture in thirds,
alternately with milk, beginning and ending with flour
mixture. Divide batter among prepared cake pans,
smoothing tops.
• Bake until a wooden pick inserted in the centers
comes out clean, approximately 20 minutes. Let cool in
pans for 10 minutes before inverting onto wire racks to
cool completely.
• Spread Chocolate-Raspberry Mousse onto tops of
all 3 cake layers. Stack layers. Spread mousse onto
sides of stacked cake.
• Transfer remaining mousse to a pastry bag fitted
with a small to medium star tip and a small round tip,
and decorate top of cake, if desired.
• Garnish sides and top center of cake with grated
chocolate, if desired. Garnish top of cake with
raspberry jelly and fresh raspberries, if desired.

Chocolate-Raspberry Mousse
Gluten-free | *Yield: 8 cups*

12 ounces bittersweet chocolate
2 ounces unsweetened chocolate
6 large eggs, separated
1 cup seedless raspberry jam
2 cups heavy whipping cream
2 tablespoons raspberry liqueur
1 tablespoon vanilla extract
¼ teaspoon cream of tartar

• In a double boiler over simmering water, melt both
chocolates. Remove from heat. Gradually add ⅓ cup
melted chocolate to egg yolks to temper, stirring
constantly. Add egg-yolk mixture to melted chocolate,
stirring well. (Chocolate mixture may harden a bit.)
Add jam, stirring well to soften chocolate mixture.
• In a large mixing bowl, combine cream, raspberry
liqueur, and vanilla extract. Beat at medium-high speed
with a mixer until medium peaks form. Refrigerate until
needed.
• In another large mixing bowl, combine egg whites
and cream of tartar. Beat at high speed with a mixer
fitted with the whisk attachment until stiff peaks form.
• Add half of egg-white mixture to chocolate mixture,
stirring well. Add remaining half, folding gently.
• Add half of whipped cream to chocolate, folding
until evenly mixed. Add remaining half, folding gently.
• Transfer mousse to a metal bowl, and cover with
plastic wrap. Refrigerate until firm and ready to use.

Editor's Note: This recipe contains raw eggs.

ROSE TREE COTTAGE
all for a decent cup of tea

If you come early for afternoon tea at Rose Tree Cottage, owner Edmund Fry may challenge you to a croquet match on the front lawn. "You've got to be a good cheat to be able to play croquet well," he points out. "It really is fun."

—⟨⟨⟨—

Rose Tree Cottage
801 S. Pasadena Avenue
Pasadena, CA 91105
626-793-3337
rosetreecottage.com

If you're looking for a truly British tea experience on the West Coast, you won't find a better one than Rose Tree Cottage in Pasadena, California. But for British expatriate Edmund Fry, who opened Rose Tree Cottage with his Oklahoma-born wife, Mary, 40 years ago, the tearoom has always been about one thing. "I opened a tearoom so I could get a decent cup of tea myself," he says simply.

From the authentic scones, made from a recipe handed down in Edmund's family for more than 100 years, to the AGA range where they are baked, Edmund says, tea at Rose Tree Cottage is completely British. Everything in the tearoom's English Village Shop is British made, and tea is served on Royal Crown Derby and Royal Doulton china by British servers.

"The only thing that's not British is the cat," Edmund says with a smile. "She's an American."

When patrons arrive for afternoon tea, Edmund greets them impeccably dressed in a white dinner jacket or perhaps full tails. Thoughtful guests will have made a reservation at least a week in advance, although the Frys try to accommodate anyone who walks in without one. "I try to leave a couple of tables open," Edmund says. "We never know when the British consulate may call to say there's a royal in town." Over the years, the tearoom has played host to Prince Charles, as well as Will and Kate, the Duke and Duchess of Cambridge.

Tea begins with an elderflower cordial. "It's a favorite of Her Majesty, the Queen," Edmund points out. "We serve it chilled with a raspberry. That's the way Her Majesty likes it."

This nonalcoholic aperitif is followed by never-ending loose-leaf English Village Tea, Rose Tree Cottage's mellow house blend of Ceylon and Indian that Edmund created when the tearoom opened.

"We follow that with roast beef and Yorkshire pudding and a selection of finger sandwiches—everything from English cucumber to Scottish salmon," Edmund says. Scones are served next, in the British fashion, with Devonshire cream, Rose Tree Cottage's own jams, and lemon curd, made fresh on the premises each day. The final course includes an assortment of desserts, and more than one guest leaves with a packet of leftovers.

"What I love about what we do is our wonderful eclectic clientele," says Mary, who was raised drinking hot tea in Oklahoma with her Scottish grandmother. "We've seen children grow up and bring their children to the tearoom. It's been a fantastic life."

Edmund agrees that owning a British tearoom in California has been a wonderful experience. "If we had opened the same place in England, it wouldn't have been the same," he says. He would never have met Margaret Thatcher or General Norman Schwarzkopf, not to mention the cast of the PBS television series *Downton Abbey*. "Royalty has literally come to us."

More importantly, Edmund says, Rose Tree Cottage has been the engine that drives the Bloom Where Planted program, a charity he and Mary founded in Africa 20 years ago. The couple rebuilt and support a local school in Kenya that now has 800 students. "We board them, we feed them, we clothe them," Edmund explains. "What makes me happy about Rose Tree is that we've managed to change children's lives."

Tea at Rose Tree Cottage in Pasadena, California, is a truly British experience. Everything—from the china on the tables to the Plum Cake (below), a recipe handed down from Mary Fry's Scottish grandmother—hails from the British Isles.

(Recipe is on page 90.)

Recipes courtesy of Rose Tree Cottage

Egg and Watercress Finger Sandwiches
Yield: 16

6 hard-cooked eggs, peeled and finely chopped
1 generous tablespoon mayonnaise
⅛ teaspoon ground celery seed
⅛ teaspoon onion powder
⅛ teaspoon salt
4 slices wheat bread
4 slices white bread
Unsalted butter, softened
Watercress

• In a bowl, combine chopped eggs, mayonnaise, celery seed, onion powder, and salt, stirring to blend.
• Spread bread slices with a thin coat of butter. Divide egg mixture among wheat bread slices, butter side up. Top egg salad layer with watercress. Top watercress layer with white bread slices, butter side down.
• Using a bread knife, trim and discard crusts from sandwiches. Cut each sandwich into 4 (1-inch) fingers.

Crab Pinwheels
Yield: 24

1 (8-ounce) container fresh pasteurized crabmeat
1 (6-ounce) can crabmeat
½ cup unsalted butter, softened
1 tablespoon apple brandy, such as Calvados
1 tablespoon fresh lemon juice
½ teaspoon salt
¼ teaspoon ground white pepper
1 unsliced loaf wheat bread
Garnish: caviar

• In the work bowl of a food processor, combine crabmeat, butter, apple brandy, lemon juice, salt, and pepper. Pulse until smooth.
• Trim crusts from bread loaf. Cut 4 (¼-inch-thick) lengthwise slices from loaf. To make bread more pliable, lay slices on damp paper towels.
• Spread crab mixture onto bread slices. Beginning at a short end, roll each slice into a pinwheel. Wrap each roll in plastic wrap, and refrigerate until firm, approximately 30 minutes.
• Just before serving, cut each roll into 6 slices.
• Garnish with fresh caviar, if desired.

Plum Cake

(photo on page 88)
Yield: 8 to 12 servings

1 cup cold, brewed black tea
½ cup unsalted butter
1 cup golden raisins and currants, mixed together
    (approximately ½ cup each)
1 cup chopped prunes
1 cup dark muscovado sugar*
2 cups self-rising flour
1 teaspoon baking soda
Garnish: caster sugar

• Preheat oven to 350°.
• Coat an 8-inch round (3-inch deep preferred) cake
pan with butter. Line pan with parchment paper.
• In a saucepan, combine tea, butter, golden raisins,
currants, prunes, and muscovado sugar, and bring to
a boil over medium heat, stirring occasionally. Reduce
heat to low, and simmer for 3 to 5 minutes. Remove
from heat, and let mixture cool completely.
• In a small bowl, combine flour and baking soda,
whisking well. Add to cooled fruit mixture, stirring
until thoroughly combined. Transfer batter to
prepared cake pan.
• Bake on the middle shelf of oven until a wooden
pick inserted in the center of cake comes out clean,
45 to 60 minutes. Let cool in pan for 10 minutes.
Remove from cake pan, and let cool completely
on a wire cooling rack.
• Garnish top of cake with a dusting of caster sugar,
if desired.
• Store in an airtight container at room temperature.

*Muscovado sugar is a minimally processed dark brown
sugar with a strong molasses taste.*

Miniature Lemon Swiss Rolls

Yield: 16 to 20 servings

1 cup unbleached all-purpose flour
½ teaspoon baking powder
4 large eggs
½ cup plus 1 tablespoon caster sugar
    (superfine granulated sugar), divided
1 tablespoon water
2 (8-ounce) jars prepared lemon curd*
Garnish: additional caster sugar, fresh rose petals

• Preheat oven to 425°.
• Line a 16x10-inch baking pan with buttered
parchment paper.

• In a small bowl, combine flour and baking powder,
whisking well.
• In a large bowl, combine eggs and ½ cup caster
sugar, and beat with the whisk attachment of a mixer
until mixture is thick and creamy, 4 to 5 minutes. Add
flour mixture, folding to incorporate. Add water, stirring
to combine. Pour batter into prepared pan, smoothing
top with a spatula.
• Bake until top springs back when lightly touched,
5 to 10 minutes.
• Lay a piece of parchment paper on a work surface,
and sprinkle it with remaining 1 tablespoon caster sugar.
When cake is done, turn it out onto prepared parchment
paper. Remove and discard parchment paper that was
lining cake pan. Trim and discard edges from cake layer.
Cut cake and prepared parchment into 4 rectangles,
making one cut lengthwise and one cut crosswise.
• Beginning at a short end, gently roll up each cake
piece with its parchment paper. Wrap each roll in a
clean, warm, damp cloth. Let cool on a wire rack,
seam side down.
• Once cooled, gently unroll each cake piece. Spread
a thin layer of lemon curd onto cake, and reroll without
parchment paper. Refrigerate, tightly sealed, until
needed.
• Garnish rolls with a dusting of caster sugar, if desired.
• Cut each roll into ½-inch slices.
• Garnish slices with fresh rose petals, if desired.

*We used English Village Lemon Curd available only
from Rose Tree Cottage, 626-793-3337.*

ROYAL PARK HOTEL
a personal touch

Tables adorned with detailed decorative touches tell guests that a gracious afternoon-tea service awaits at the Royal Park Hotel.

Royal Park Hotel
600 East University
Rochester, MI 48307
248-453-8698
royalparkhotel.net

The Royal Park Hotel sits on an extensive estate in downtown Rochester, Michigan. Since opening in September 2004, the locally owned English manor–style boutique hotel has attracted tea lovers from near and far. From the beginning, it has offered a first-class tea experience—each guest is treated like family, and every visit is a special event. The by-reservation-only tea service is available Wednesday through Sunday from 2:00 to 4:00 p.m.

The hotel's library is a relaxing space where afternoon-tea guests wait until their setting is ready. Tea Hostess Mary Kuhn arrives to usher each party to the sunny Gallery Room where tea tables are arranged overlooking scenic Paint Creek. Once seated, guests are presented with the current tea collection and given an opportunity to smell each choice before making a final decision. After a detailed explanation of the tea table, the group settles in for an afternoon of exceptional service, quality tea, and delightful food.

The Royal Park Hotel offers an all-inclusive regal afternoon-tea experience. The package includes a choice of a Kir Royale cocktail or sparkling cider, as well as six tea sandwiches, English fruit scones with clotted cream and lemon curd, six sweets, hot hors d'oeuvres, and the guest's tea selection. The tea menu features 10 loose selections from California-based Mighty Leaf Tea. Some of the most popular are Pear Caramel, Green Tea Passion Fruit, and Masala Chocolate Truffle. Each pot of tea is prepared with precision and delivered with a ribbon label to note the flavor. Guests are particularly fond of the phyllo cup with hickory-smoked chicken and fruit chutney; the rosemary profiteroles with roast beef, cheddar, and horseradish cream; the warm scones; the shortbread cookies; and the dark chocolate decadence pastry.

The delivery of hot hors d'oeuvres signals the last interlude before the hotel staff step back, though still watching for any arising need, and allow guests to enjoy the table's bounty at their own pace.

Each guest takes home a complimentary doily-lined box filled with leftover treats. These "care packages" represent the level of attention that goes into each afternoon-tea experience. Mary notes, "Visitors arrive as guests, stay as friends, and they leave as family."

A personal touch is incorporated into every part of the tea experience—from the table dressings to the fine china. Mary keeps a detailed account of each guest or party, noting previous table settings, tea wares, and personal food preferences. Tablescapes, as well as the signature tea, food, and service, are tailored on each subsequent visit so patrons experience something new. This unique standard has garnered a loyal customer base of locals and visitors who consistently refer other afternoon-tea connoisseurs to the hotel. Mary says they strive to "wow guests by providing a relaxed and pampered afternoon in an environment created just for them with a focus on gracious, silent service."

The Royal Park's quiet mission to impress "Every Guest, Every Time" rings a bit truer each time someone leaves with a doily-lined care package.

Appealing three-tiered trays filled with petite sweets, savories, and scones line picturesque tables arranged with beautiful place settings, soft linens, and lovely tea wares. The culinary team utilizes a variety of local, garden-fresh produce to create each seasonal menu.

Courtesy of Royal Park Hotel

- Preheat oven to 350°.
- Line 2 rimmed baking sheets with parchment paper.
- In the bowl of a stand mixer, combine flour, granulated sugar, baking powder, and salt, stirring at low speed with the paddle attachment to blend. Add butter to flour mixture, mixing at low speed until it resembles coarse crumbs.
- Add 2¼ cups cream, mixing just until a dough forms.
- Turn out dough onto a lightly floured surface. Sprinkle currants and raisins over dough, and knead gently 4 to 5 times to incorporate.
- Using a rolling pin, roll dough to a ½-inch thickness. Using a 2¼-inch round cutter, cut 26 scones from dough, rerolling scraps as necessary. Place scones 2 inches apart on prepared baking sheets.
- In a small bowl, combine egg and remaining 1 tablespoon cream, whisking well to make an eggwash. Brush tops of scones lightly with eggwash, and sprinkle with turbinado sugar.
- Bake until scones are golden brown and a wooden pick inserted in the centers comes out clean, approximately 20 minutes.

Smoked Salmon BLTs
Yield: 12

6 slices rye bread
1 tablespoon olive oil
2 slices bacon, cooked crisp and finely chopped
¼ cup mayonnaise
1 (4-ounce) package sliced smoked salmon
12 Campari tomato slices
½ cup thinly sliced Romaine lettuce

- Preheat oven to 350°.
- Line a rimmed baking sheet with parchment paper.
- Using a 2-inch round cutter, cut 2 shapes from each bread slice. Place rounds on prepared baking sheet, and drizzle with olive oil.
- Bake for 6 minutes. Let cool.
- In a bowl, combine bacon and mayonnaise. Spread onto toasted bread slices.
- Layer smoked salmon, tomato slices, and lettuce on 6 bread slices. Top with remaining bread slices, mayonnaise side down.

English Fruit Scones
Yield: 26

3¾ cups plus 2 tablespoons all-purpose flour
¼ cup granulated sugar
2 tablespoons baking powder
2 teaspoons salt
¾ cup cold unsalted butter, cut into small pieces
2¼ cups plus 1 tablespoon heavy whipping cream, divided
¾ cups dried currants
¾ cups raisins
1 large egg
1 tablespoon turbinado sugar

Hickory-Smoked Chicken Salad in Phyllo Cups with Apricot Chutney
Yield: 15

¼ cup finely chopped dried apricots
2 tablespoons rice wine vinegar
1 tablespoon sugar
1 cup chopped smoked chicken
2 tablespoons mayonnaise
1 teaspoon chopped chives
1 (1.9-ounce) package mini phyllo cups
Garnish: almond slices

• In a small saucepan, combine apricots, vinegar, and sugar. Cook over medium heat until bubbling, 2 to 3 minutes. Remove apricot chutney from heat, and let cool.
• In a medium bowl, combine chicken, mayonnaise, and chives, stirring to blend. Divide chicken mixture among phyllo cups.
• Top each phyllo cup with apricot chutney.
• Garnish with almond slices, if desired.

Cucumber Canapés
Yield: 6

2 tablespoons creamy-style Boursin cheese,
    at room temperature
2 slices white bread
1 English cucumber
Garnish: mayonnaise, microgreens

• Spread Boursin cheese onto bread slices.
• Using a knife or a large vegetable peeler, cut 10 long ribbons from cucumber.
• Cut 5 cucumber ribbons in half crosswise to yield 10 pieces of equal length. Place pieces on Boursin side of a bread slice, overlapping evenly to fit. Trim bread crusts and edges of cucumber to form a square, and cut square into 3 rectangular canapés. Repeat with remaining cucumber ribbons and bread slice.
• Garnish each canapé with a dollop of mayonnaise and microgreens, if desired.

THE ST. JAMES TEAROOM
a theatre of tea

Although The St. James Tearoom offers a traditional English tea service, the façade of the building reflects Albuquerque's Spanish heritage, in keeping with the city's zoning laws.

The St. James Tearoom
320 Osuna Road NE,
Building D
Albuquerque, NM 87107
505-242-3752
stjamestearoom.com

There's a bit of Britain tucked into the New Mexico desert just north of downtown Albuquerque. It is an oasis of tea in a dry and thirsty land. And while diners at cafes down the road debate their preference for green or red chiles on an enchilada, guests of The St. James Tearoom ponder the protocol for dabbing clotted cream or lemon curd onto a warm scone. Anglophiles find here all the things they love about the motherland—literature, music, art, manners—infused into a teatime setting that is, simply said, more British than Britain.

The artist who conceived the idea of opening an English tearoom in this unlikely part of the world is Mary Alice Higbie. A classically trained Japanese-porcelain painter, she approached the creation of her tea business with an artistic spirit. Although Mary Alice has been a tea lover from an early age, she prepared for her business venture by visiting countless British tea establishments and receiving training through Dorothea Johnson's tea and etiquette certification program.

The St. James Tearoom opened on December 22, 1999, with two employees, and Mary Alice's business took off immediately. Within six months, this tea haven received a four-star rating from the *Albuquerque Journal* and the title "Best New Restaurant" in Albuquerque by *La Cocinita* magazine.

It wasn't long before the budding tea entrepreneur realized she needed more hands, and her son Daniel volunteered to become general manager. Equipped with a Master of Arts in International Relations and a bit of British flair from his time as an exchange student at Oxford University, the savvy son added a masculine influence not often seen in American tearooms. For instance, his annual Cigar Tea, held outdoors on the patio, is a much-anticipated event that always sells out quickly.

The immediate charm of this theatre of tea is the layout of the dining areas. Mary Alice has set nine private alcoves, or "nooks" as she calls them, to resemble British parlors, with

names like Munstead Wood, Newstead Abbey, or Beatrix Potter's Hill Top Farm. A spacious center library accommodates large gatherings, or it can be partitioned into curtained hideaways. Each setting is furnished with stuffed chairs or sofas and accented with low tables, antique lamps, Victorian books, and bric-a-brac reminiscent of a 19th-century British home. Servers, dressed in period costume and well scripted in their presentations, add an authentic touch to this theatrical stage.

And a busy stage it is as an endless array of theatrical and musical events unfold here. Teatime performances have included "An Evening with Jane Austen," Victorian poetry readings, Shakespearean plays, and murder mysteries. Afternoon tea is a bounteous meal presented in courses, beginning with the arrival of the ubiquitous Edwardian three-tiered tray. An assortment of savories and tea sandwiches, St. James traditional cream scones, and a variety of sweets and desserts all are handmade on-site by the chef. (Both vegetarian and gluten-free options are available with advance notice.) The teatime menu changes monthly, with new creations reflecting the theme of the season or the theatrical event about to unfold.

Guests of The St. James access the dining areas through a labyrinth of tea wares known as The St. James Market. One of the most complete tearoom gift shops in America, it stocks an array of beautiful tea things, as well as a comprehensive selection of fine-quality loose teas, including its signature Higbie and Sons Teas.

From the beginning of their tea adventure, one mission of Mary Alice and Daniel Higbie has been to feed the soul as well as the body. Judging by the smiles on their guests' faces, this dynamic mother-and-son duo have certainly met that goal.

(Recipe is on page 101.)

At The St. James Tearoom, owner Mary Alice Higbie and her son and general manager, Daniel, pictured at top right, have created a theatre of tea that reflects their mutual love of Great Britain and its tea traditions.

Courtesy of The St. James Tearoom

- Preheat oven 350°.
- Line a rimmed baking sheet with parchment paper.
- In a large bowl, combine flour, almond flour, sugar, baking powder, and salt, whisking well. Using a pastry blender, cut butter into flour mixture until it resembles coarse crumbs.
- In a liquid-measuring cup, combine cream, rose water, almond extract, and food coloring. Add to flour mixture, stirring until mixture is evenly moist. (If dough seems dry, add more cream, 1 tablespoon at a time.) Working gently, bring mixture together with hands until a dough forms.
- Turn out dough onto a lightly floured surface. Knead gently a few times. Using a rolling pin, roll out dough to a ⅝-inch thickness. Using a 2½-inch heart-shaped cookie cutter, cut 16 scones from dough, rerolling scraps no more than twice. Place scones 2 inches apart on prepared baking sheet.
- Bake until scones are lightly browned, 14 to 16 minutes.

Basil-Corn Pepper Cups
Gluten-free | (*photo on page 100*)
Yield: 30

3 cups frozen corn kernels, thawed
½ cup minced red onion
⅓ cup diced fresh basil
3 tablespoons apple cider vinegar
3 tablespoons olive oil
½ teaspoon salt
½ teaspoon ground black pepper
15 fresh baby peppers, halved, veined,
    and seeded

- In a large bowl, combine corn, onion, and basil.
- In another bowl, combine vinegar, olive oil, salt, and pepper, whisking until emulsified. Pour vinaigrette over corn mixture, stirring to coat.
- Cut a small slice from bottoms of peppers to ensure they do not tip over. Fill peppers with corn mixture.

Rose-Almond Scones
Yield: 16

2½ cups all-purpose flour
1 cup plus 1 tablespoon almond flour
½ cup sugar
1 tablespoon baking powder
1 teaspoon salt
6 tablespoons cold salted butter, cut into pieces
1¼ cups heavy whipping cream
3 tablespoons rose water
2 teaspoons almond extract
⅛ teaspoon red food coloring

Jane's Chocolate Indulgence
Gluten-free | *Yield: 24 servings*

1 cup unsalted butter
4 ounces unsweetened chocolate, chopped
2 cups sugar, divided
½ cup cornstarch
¼ cup almond flour
¼ cup tapioca flour
¼ cup glutinous rice flour*
1¼ teaspoons guar gum
1 teaspoon kosher salt
5 large eggs
2¼ teaspoons vanilla extract
1 recipe Truffle Frosting (recipe follows)
¼ cup white chocolate morsels
¼ cup semisweet chocolate morsels
2 teaspoons all-vegetable shortening, divided

• Preheat oven to 350°.
• Spray a 13x9-inch baking sheet with cooking spray, line with parchment paper, and spray again.
• In a large heatproof bowl set over a saucepan with 2 inches of barely simmering water (don't let bowl touch water), melt butter and chocolate, being careful not to let chocolate scorch. Add 1 cup sugar, whisking to blend. Remove saucepan from heat, and set aside.
• In a medium bowl, combine cornstarch, almond flour, tapioca flour, rice flour, guar gum, and salt, whisking to blend.
• In a large mixing bowl, combine eggs and remaining 1 cup sugar. Beat at medium-high speed with a mixer fitted with a whisk attachment until mixture doubles in volume.
• Add egg mixture to melted chocolate, alternately with flour mixture, stirring until batter resembles chocolate pudding. Add vanilla extract, stirring to blend.
• Spread batter evenly into prepared baking sheet.
• Bake until cake is set in the middle, 28 to 30 minutes. Remove from oven, and let cool completely in pan on a wire rack.
• Remove cake from pan, and place on a cutting board. Spread Truffle Frosting over cooled cake. Freeze cake for approximately 30 minutes.
• In the same manner as above, melt white chocolate with 1 teaspoon shortening. Separately, melt semisweet chocolate with remaining 1 teaspoon shortening.
• Stripe cake horizontally with both melted chocolates.
• Trim and discard edges of cake, running knife under hot water and wiping dry between cuts. Cut cake into 12 (2¾-inch) squares. Cut squares in half diagonally to make 24 triangles.

Glutinuous rice flour is made from short-grain, sticky rice. Regular rice flour may be substituted.

Truffle Frosting
Gluten-free | *Yield: approximately 2 cups*

1 cup semisweet chocolate morsels
1 (8-ounce) package cream cheese, softened
¼ cup confectioners' sugar
½ cup seedless raspberry jam
¼ cup coffee concentrate
¼ teaspoon salt

• Melt chocolate morsels according to package directions, and set aside to cool.
• In a large bowl, beat cream cheese until smooth. Add confectioners' sugar, beating until smooth. Add cooled chocolate, raspberry jam, coffee concentrate, and salt, beating until well combined.
• Use immediately.

TAJ BOSTON
history and honey

Teatime at Taj Boston is teeming with first-class service, delectable teas and food, cheerful toasts, and a relaxing setting for guests.

Taj Boston
15 Arlington Street
Boston, MA 02116
617-598-5255
tajhotels.com/boston

Since 1630, Boston, Massachusetts, has stood at the forefront of tradition and innovation. It is one of America's oldest cities and the site of the Boston Tea Party in 1773. People have long gathered in the City on the Hill to engage in the custom of afternoon tea, and few places are more ideally suited for it than the Taj Boston. Initially opened in 1927 as the Ritz-Carlton Boston, the hotel was renamed in 2007 after becoming part of the Taj Resorts, Hotels and Palaces portfolio.

Hotel staff usher afternoon-tea guests through the majestic gold-and-ebony-framed revolving glass door and direct them to the lavish French and Adams Rooms on the second floor. Both spaces are decorated in a traditional British style that has an air of luxury and refinement—exquisite crystal chandeliers overhead, the soft lighting of sconces, elegant drapes trimming scenic windows, picturesque paintings, and cozy sofas and tables. Sheila Hayden, Director of Sales and Marketing, says even the fragrance of the air mesmerizes guests. "The freshness of the *mignardise* and the aroma from varieties of tea released in the room gives the guest an inviting atmosphere," she says.

Service is hosted Saturday and Sunday between 1:30 and 5:00 p.m. Visitors dine on ornate china on offerings from three-tiered silver trays while the skillful bowing of a violinist or strumming of a Spanish guitarist fills the room with the masterpieces of Mozart, Beethoven, and other favorite composers. Each afternoon-tea menu selection includes a mixture of scones with Devonshire cream and lemon curd, savories, sweets, a pot of brewed tea, and a glass of prosecco. Current options include the Taj Royale Tea, the Taj Tea, the Duchess Tea, Traditional Cheese Tasting (a selection of cheeses, crackers, sliced baguette, and fruit), and the Children's Tea (peanut butter and jelly sandwiches, a chocolate chip cookie, a chocolate-covered strawberry, and a pot of hot chocolate).

The tea menu boasts 22 selections curated from a variety of global sources. Some of the most popular include White Blossom, Vanilla Earl Grey, Taj Herbal, Jasmine Pearl, and Mountain Berry. Tea specialist Anil Shrestha notes tea connoisseurs are fond of the Taj Boston's fine range available year-round. He says his tea servers pay close attention when preparing each pot of tea (using the proper temperature and steep time) and make it their duty to serve an excellent cup to each guest. The hotel also serves tea cocktails, such as Hot Toddy, Blueberry Tea, Citrus Iced Tea, and Royal Tea.

Chef Robert Alger leads the culinary team that prepares food fresh in small batches to ensure the quality of every item. Some of the most popular menu items include the smoked salmon tea sandwich served on multigrain toast with caper berries and pickled onion; chicken salad tea sandwich topped with a candied walnut; vanilla panna cotta; and dark chocolate roulade. Gluten-free, vegetarian, and vegan options are available as well.

The Taj Boston also is the home of a sustainable beekeeping site that houses 12 beehives on the hotel roof. The bee management team, Best Bees, oversees the care of 10,000 to 35,000 bees and facilitates the annual harvesting of honey. The hotel utilizes this fresh-honey supply in many of the afternoon-tea specialty desserts and tea-infused cocktails.

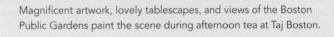

Magnificent artwork, lovely tablescapes, and views of the Boston Public Gardens paint the scene during afternoon tea at Taj Boston.

Courtesy of Taj Boston

Pistachio Macarons
Gluten-free | *Yield: 20 sandwich cookies*

150 grams (1½ cups) almond flour
150 grams (1⅓ cups plus 2 tablespoons)
   confectioners' sugar
110 grams (approximately 4) egg whites, divided
150 grams (⅔ cup plus 1½ teaspoons) granulated
   sugar
50 grams (¼ cup) water
Green paste food coloring, such as Wilton leaf green
1 recipe Pistachio Filling (recipe follows)

• In the work bowl of a food processor, combine almond flour and confectioners' sugar. Pulse until mixture is blended. Add 55 grams (2) egg whites, and pulse until mixture has the consistency of a paste.
• In the bowl of a stand mixer fitted with the whisk attachment, slowly begin beating remaining 55 grams (2) egg whites. Gradually increase speed, and beat until very soft peaks form. (Be careful not to overbeat.)
• In a saucepan, combine granulated sugar and water over medium heat, and cook until mixture registers 240° on a candy thermometer. With mixer running at medium speed, slowly add sugar syrup to beaten egg whites, pouring syrup down side of mixing bowl. Once all syrup has been added, increase mixer speed to high, and beat egg whites until very stiff peaks form, approximately 3 minutes.
• Add half of egg-white mixture to almond paste, folding to combine. Make sure first half of egg-white mixture is well incorporated before folding in remaining half of egg whites. Add a drop or two of green food coloring, if desired, and continue to fold mixture until a slow steady stream of batter falls from spatula.
• Preheat oven to 300°.
• Line 2 rimmed baking sheets with parchment paper or silicone baking mats.
• Transfer batter to a pastry bag fitted with a medium round tip. Pipe batter into 1-inch disks on prepared baking sheets. Let stand until a skin forms on macaron shells, approximately 45 minutes. (You should be able to gently rub your finger on the macaron shell without

any batter sticking to finger. Once shells reach this point, they are ready for baking.)
• Bake macarons for 6 minutes. Rotate baking sheets in oven, and bake for 5 to 6 minutes longer. (To test for doneness, gently wiggle macaron shells. If they wiggle with your finger, continue to bake for 1 to 2 minutes. If they have very little give, they are done.)
• Let macaron shells cool completely before removing from baking sheets. Pair up macaron shells of equal size.
• Place Pistachio Filling in a pastry bag fitted with a round or star tip. Pipe filling onto one half of each macaron pair, and top with remaining half.

Editor's Note: For consistent results, we recommend weighing macaron ingredients instead of using volume measurements.

Pistachio Filling
Gluten-free | *Yield: 1⅓ cups*

⅓ cup pistachios, roasted
3½ tablespoons unsalted butter, softened
1½ cups confectioners' sugar, divided
4 tablespoons all-vegetable shortening
½ teaspoon vanilla extract
1 egg white

• In the work bowl of a food processor, finely grind pistachios.
• In a mixing bowl, combine butter and ¾ cup confectioners' sugar, beating at medium speed with a mixer fitted with a paddle attachment until smooth and creamy. Scrape bowl well. Add shortening, vanilla extract, and remaining ¾ cup confectioners' sugar. Beat until light and airy.
• Replace paddle attachment of mixer with whisk attachment. With mixer at medium speed, slowly add egg white to butter mixture. Continue beating until filling is light and airy.
• Add ground pistachios to filling, folding gently to blend.

Editor's Note: This recipe contains raw eggs.

Pomegranate Panna Cotta
Gluten-free | *Yield: 11 (4-ounce) servings*

2 (¼-ounce) envelopes unflavored gelatin, divided
4 tablespoons cold water, divided
3½ cups heavy whipping cream
2 tablespoons plus 2 teaspoons sugar
½ vanilla bean, split lengthwise and seeds scraped
   and reserved
1¼ cups pomegranate juice
¼ cup pomegranate arils

• In a small bowl, sprinkle gelatin from 1 envelope over
2 tablespoons cold water. Let stand for 1 minute.
• In a saucepan, combine cream and sugar, whisking
to blend. Add reserved vanilla bean seeds. Cook over
medium heat until steaming. Add gelatin, whisking
until it dissolves completely.
• Divide cream mixture among 11 (4-ounce) glasses,
leaving room at the top for gelée. Refrigerate until set,
approximately 4 hours.
• In another small bowl, sprinkle gelatin from remaining 1 envelope over remaining 2 tablespoons cold
water. Let stand for 1 minute.
• In a saucepan, heat pomegranate juice over
medium heat until steaming. Add gelatin, whisking
until it dissolves completely. Let cool to room
temperature before using.
• Sprinkle pomegranate arils on each panna cotta, and
top evenly with gelée. Refrigerate until set, approximately 1 hour.

Hazelnut Spice Cookies
Gluten-free | *Yield: approximately 80*

4½ cups plus ⅓ cup hazelnut flour
1½ cups plus 1 tablespoon granulated sugar
2½ cups confectioners' sugar, divided
2 teaspoons ground cinnamon
½ teaspoon fresh lemon zest
4 egg whites, divided

• In the mixing bowl of a stand mixer fitted with a
paddle attachment, combine hazelnut flour, granulated
sugar, ½ cup confectioners' sugar, cinnamon, and lemon
zest, beating at lowest speed to blend. Slowly add
3 egg whites, and beat until dough comes together.
• Turn out dough onto a sheet of parchment paper.
Using a rolling pin, roll dough to a ¼-inch thickness.
Slide parchment paper onto a baking sheet, and freeze
for 2 hours.
• In a medium bowl, combine remaining 2 cups confectioners' sugar and remaining egg white, whisking
until smooth. Spread onto frozen dough, and return to
freezer for 2 hours.
• Preheat oven to 425°.
• Spray several rimmed baking sheets with cooking
spray.
• Remove dough from freezer, and cut into 1-inch
squares. Place cookies 1 inch apart on prepared baking
sheets.
• Bake until lightly browned, approximately 6 minutes.
Transfer cookies to wire racks, and let cool completely.

TEABERRY'S TEA ROOM
a family affair

Left, The Salon, Teaberry's largest room, is on the tearoom's main floor, along with The Garden Room. A wonderful array of teas and gifts await in Teaberry's Carriage House, above.

Teaberry's Tea Room
2 Main Street
Flemington, NJ 08822
908-788-1010
teaberrys.com

A beautifully imposing early 19th-century house at the corner of Main Street and Pennsylvania Avenue is home to Teaberry's Tea Room. Realizing the community needed a place people could get together for conversation and good food, Susan Peterson founded the tearoom in historic Flemington, New Jersey, in 2004. For its first five years, Teaberry's was in a much smaller building, but when the opportunity to move to its current 100-seat, handicap-accessible location presented itself, Susan jumped at the chance. "Everyday, I can't wait to get here—even after all these years," she says.

The rooms of the lovely two-story facility lend themselves to celebrations of all sorts, including children's parties. The size of the group, as well as guests' mobility, often dictates which of the six rooms can accommodate them. "When someone is making a reservation, we ask them immediately, 'Can you go upstairs?'" says Susan. The second floor's four rooms are smaller than those on the main floor. Each has a different color scheme or theme. The Greenwood Room is decorated with dark colors and fruit-embellished china. Adjacent to it is the Miss Teaberry Room, which has an Asian theme in keeping with the origins of tea. The golden-hued Regency Room, across the hall, houses Susan's collection of commemorative English china. Done mostly in pinks and blacks, the French-inspired Fleur-de-lis Room is the smallest on that floor and features pretty Limoges china. Patrons have easy access to the tearoom's vintage hats, which fill the upstairs bathtub and are displayed on hat stands. Young guests—and the young at heart—enjoy selecting a hat to wear during teatime.

"Children of all ages are welcome," says Susan. "If we don't teach them, how else will they learn to behave?"

Teaberry's, which boasts a full lunch menu in addition to that of afternoon tea, is closed only on Mondays. Reservations for lunch or afternoon tea are strongly recommended. Customers can choose from an array of afternoon-tea options such as Lady Astor's Cream Tea, which includes two scones with lemon curd, clotted cream, and preserves. "We always have three types of scones, and one is always plain," explains Susan. The other two flavors change weekly and typically include an option with nuts and one without. The four-course Milady's Tea features eight different tea sandwiches (the cucumber one is a staple), a choice of scone with requisite condiments, eight petite sweets, plus sorbet or gelato. "There is always something chocolate, and we always have our lemon bar." Otherwise, Susan says, everything changes.

Teatime offerings naturally include a pot of hot tea, selected from an impressive list of 125 teas. These loose-leaf teas are also available for purchase in the tearoom's adjacent Carriage House Boutique, which is overflowing with wonderful teacentric accoutrements and gifts Susan sources.

Teaberry's is certainly a family affair. Susan's husband, Andrew, takes care of the tearoom's payables and receivables, and their son, Christopher, does the bulk of the grocery shopping. Daughter Sara worked at the tearoom during high school and now serves as hostess, manages the front of the house, and handles payroll, among other responsibilities. "She works as much as I do, which is more than fulltime," says Susan. "She is the one booking the parties, and she is wonderful at remembering customers' names."

The family-friendly atmosphere, delicious food, extensive tea list, and elegant setting keep customers coming back time after time, hopeful this tearoom will be a fixture in Flemington for generations to come.

It Takes A Long
To Grow An Old Fr[...]

Although an upside-down Christmas tree is a Victorian tradition, the one at Teaberry's was hung that way for a very practical reason—to allow room for people to walk by. A popular spot for pictures, the tree stays up year-round. "We just change the decorations with the seasons," says Susan Peterson, pictured above with her daughter, Sara.

The RECIPES

Courtesy of Teaberry's Tea Room

- In a large bowl, combine flour, ¾ cup sugar, baking powder, salt, and baking soda, whisking well. Using a pastry blender, cut butter into flour mixture until it resembles coarse crumbs.
- Add blueberries and lavender, tossing to combine.
- In a liquid-measuring cup, combine 1 cup buttermilk and vanilla extract. Add to flour mixture, stirring until mixture comes together. (If dough seems dry, add more buttermilk, 1 tablespoon at a time, until dough is uniformly moist.) Working gently, bring mixture together with hands until a dough forms.
- Turn out dough onto a lightly floured surface. Knead lightly 3 to 4 times. Using a rolling pin, roll dough to a ½-inch thickness. Using a 2½-inch round cutter, cut 14 scones from dough, rerolling scraps as needed. Place scones 2 inches apart on prepared baking sheet.
- Brush scones with remaining 1 tablespoon buttermilk, and sprinkle with remaining 1 teaspoon sugar.
- Bake until scones are golden brown and a wooden pick inserted in the centers comes out clean, 14 to 19 minutes, rotating baking sheet halfway through.
- Serve warm.

Apricot-Orange Shortbread Bars
Yield: 16 to 32

1 cup apricot preserves
1 tablespoon orange liqueur, such as Grand Marnier
1 cup unsalted butter, softened
¾ cup sugar
1 teaspoon almond extract
2 cups all-purpose flour
¼ teaspoon salt
¼ cup firmly packed almond paste, crumbled
½ cup sliced almonds, divided

- Preheat oven to 325°.
- Coat a 9-inch square cake pan with butter, and line with parchment paper, letting paper hang over sides. Coat parchment paper with butter.
- In a small bowl, combine apricot preserves and liqueur, stirring to blend.
- In a large mixing bowl, combine butter and sugar, beating at medium-high speed with a mixer until well blended. Add almond extract, beating to combine.
- In another bowl, combine flour and salt, whisking well. Add to butter mixture, beating just until incorporated.

Lavender-Blueberry Scones
Yield: 14

3 cups all-purpose flour
¾ cup plus 1 teaspoon sugar, divided
1 tablespoon baking powder
1 teaspoon salt
½ teaspoon baking soda
¾ cup cold unsalted butter, cut into pieces
½ cup fresh blueberries
1 tablespoon dry lavender buds
1 cup plus 1 tablespoon whole buttermilk, divided
1 teaspoon vanilla extract

- Preheat oven to 375°.
- Line a rimmed baking sheet with parchment paper.

- Transfer 1 cup dough to another bowl. To that dough, add almond paste, mixing with fingers until small clumps form. Add ¼ cup almonds to almond paste mixture. Set mixture aside for topping.
- Press remainder of dough into prepared pan. Spread apricot mixture evenly over dough. Sprinkle almond topping over apricot layer. Press topping lightly into apricot layer. Sprinkle with remaining ¼ cup almonds.
- Bake until topping is light golden brown and apricot layer is bubbly, 50 to 60 minutes. Let cool completely in pan on rack.
- Using parchment paper overhang, lift shortbread from pan, and place on a cutting board. Cut into bars or triangles.

Chocolate-Raspberry Bars
Yield: 12

10 ounces semisweet or bittersweet chocolate, chopped
¾ cup unsalted butter, cut into pieces
⅓ cup seedless raspberry jam
1 cup sugar
5 large eggs
⅓ cup all-purpose flour
1 teaspoon baking powder
1 recipe Chocolate-Raspberry Glaze (recipe follows)
2 tablespoons natural unsweetened cocoa powder
Garnish: fresh raspberries, fresh mint sprigs

- Preheat oven to 350°.
- Line a 9-inch square cake pan with aluminum foil. Coat foil with butter, and dust with flour.
- In a saucepan, combine chocolate and butter. Melt over low heat, stirring until smooth. Add jam, and whisk until jam melts. Let cool.
- In a large bowl, combine sugar and eggs. Beat at high speed with a mixer until thick, approximately 6 minutes.
- Sift flour and baking powder over egg mixture, and fold in. Gradually fold in chocolate mixture. Pour batter into prepared pan.
- Bake until top of cake is slightly crusty, approximately 45 minutes. Let cool a little. If there are any raised edges, press them down. Let cool completely in pan.
- Invert onto a cutting board, and peel off foil. Trim edges, if you like.
- Spread Chocolate-Raspberry Glaze over top of cake. Place in refrigerator until glaze sets, approximately 10 minutes.
- Dust cake with cocoa powder before cutting into bars or wedges.
- Garnish individual servings with raspberries and mint sprigs, if desired.

Chocolate-Raspberry Glaze
Gluten-free | Yield: approximately ¾ cup

¼ cup heavy whipping cream
¼ cup seedless raspberry jam
6 ounces semisweet or bittersweet chocolate, chopped

- In a saucepan, combine cream and raspberry jam over medium heat until jam melts and mixture comes to a boil. Remove from heat, and add chocolate, stirrring until chocolate melts. Let cool for approximately 15 minutes so mixture is spreadable but not set.

WILLARD INTERCONTINENTAL
tea and cherry blossoms

Three-tiered trays filled with a
fine selection of scones, savories,
and sweets dazzle guests in
Peacock Alley at The Willard.

Willard InterContinental
1401 Pennsylvania Avenue NW
Washington, DC 20004
202-628-9100
washington.intercontinental.com

Less than a six-minute walk from the White House, on Pennsylvania Avenue, you will find the Willard InterContinental Washington, D.C., often referred to as the Crown Jewel of the Avenue. The hotel, which dates from 1818, is simply known as The Willard and is a mélange of historic charm, modern-day lavishness, and high-class hospitality. The Willard is praised as one of the nation's most elite hotels and has hosted almost every U.S. president, beginning with Franklin Pierce in 1853. Since the 1880s, the hotel's afternoon-tea tradition has flourished, and many tea lovers say it is the best in Washington.

The hotel's impressive entrance boasts marble pillars, ornate ceilings, gilded chandeliers, and exquisite floral displays, and gracious hosts welcome all who enter. Upon arriving, guests are led from the grand lobby to the hotel's acclaimed Peacock Alley, a lengthy hallway that runs through the main level. During the early 20th century, the alley served as a place to sit and to be seen. Today, inviting tables and chairs line the space where people assemble for tea, delicacies on three-tiered trays, intimate conversation, and the soothing sounds of harp music. The hotel delights visitors with three afternoon-tea seasons: Cherry Blossom Afternoon Tea (during the National Cherry Blossom Festival between Thursday and Sunday each week), Holiday Afternoon Tea (held daily in December), and regular afternoon tea (during the rest of the year between Friday and Sunday each week).

In 1860, The Willard hosted Japan's first delegation to the United States. Beginning in 2006, the hotel has devoted an entire season each year to an expertly curated Cherry Blossom Afternoon Tea concurrent with the National Cherry Blossom Festival to salute its history with Japan. During the Cherry Blossom season, the standard live musical entertainment of the harp is traded for that of a traditional Japanese koto; elaborate

Western floral arrangements are exchanged for Japanese cherry blossoms; Eastern flavors are infused into the tea menu; and a diverse mixture of programs is presented to promote traditional Japanese art and culture. The Cherry Blossom Tea menu has featured many items including morello cherry and chocolate trifle, shiitake mushroom teriyaki glaze on brioche, matcha green tea scones, cherry curd, and ginger Devonshire cream.

Executive Chef Serge Devesa says the culinary team carefully crafts food from seasonal ingredients to ensure quality and appraises taste before placing it on the menu. He also says appearance is important. "We keep a standard to make sure the food looks lovely and is well presented." The culinary team also accommodates all dietary needs including gluten-free, vegetarian, vegan, and various allergy-sensitive diets.

The Willard exclusively serves Ronnefeldt tea, along with a variety of custom blends. The menu features 21 tea selections—everything from Earl Grey to Pai Mu Tan Silver and Cherry Blossom (a custom blend of delicate black teas and Ceylon wild cherry flavor) to Ginger and Herbs. Guests can also order a variety of cocktails, champagne, or one of its three cherry blossom–themed specialty cocktails.

Jason Deville, Executive Assistant Manager of Food and Beverage, says the team meticulously puts each element of the tea experience together: "Everything including the table linens, china, floral arrangements, menu, beverages, and entertainment is selected to create an excellent tea experience." The Willard takes pride in the service it provides. No detail is overlooked, and the brilliance shines through all elements of the tea experience, especially during cherry-blossom season.

(Recipe is on page 120.)

Soft pink Japanese cherry blossom floral arrangements color The Willard's interior to highlight the annual Cherry Blossom Afternoon Tea festivities.

The RECIPES

Courtesy of Jason Jimenez, Pastry Chef at the Willard InterContinental Washington, D.C.

- In a liquid-measuring cup, combine ¾ cup plus 3 tablespoons cream and 2 eggs, whisking well. Add to flour mixture, stirring until mixture is evenly moist. (If dough seems dry, add more cream, 1 tablespoon at a time.) Working gently, bring mixture together with hands until a dough forms.
- Turn out dough onto a rimmed baking sheet, and flatten. Wrap well with plastic wrap, and refrigerate 6 to 8 hours.
- Preheat oven to 350°.
- Line another rimmed baking sheet with parchment paper.
- On a lightly floured surface, roll out dough to a 1-inch thickness. Using a 2½-inch round cutter, cut 12 scones from dough, rerolling scraps as necessary. Place scones 2 inches apart on prepared baking sheet.*
- In a small bowl, combine remaining 1 egg and remaining 1 tablespoon cream, whisking well to make an eggwash. Brush tops of scones with eggwash.
- Bake until scones are lightly golden and a little soft in the center, approximately 20 minutes. (Be careful not to overbake scones, or they will become too dry.) Let cool slightly.
- Garnish scones with a sprinkle of confectioners' sugar just before serving, if desired.

At this point, scones can be frozen. Transfer frozen scones to an airtight container, and freeze for up to 4 days.

Editor's Note: *Serve Green Tea Scones with Cherry Curd and clotted cream.*

Green Tea Scones
Yield: 12

4 cups all-purpose flour
½ cup granulated sugar
8 teaspoons Matcha green tea powder
1 tablespoon baking powder
1 teaspoon salt
¾ cup cold unsalted butter, cut into 1-inch pieces
1 cup cold heavy whipping cream, divided
3 large eggs, divided
Garnish: confectioners' sugar

- In a large bowl, combine flour, sugar, Matcha, baking powder, and salt, whisking well. Using a pastry blender, cut butter into flour mixture until it resembles coarse crumbs.

Cherry Curd
Gluten-free | *Yield: 2 cups*

1 (300-gram) container frozen cherry puree, thawed*
½ cup unsalted butter
⅔ cup sugar, divided
4 egg yolks
3 tablespoons cornstarch

- In a large saucepan, combine puree, butter, and ⅓ cup sugar. Bring to a boil over medium heat, stirring occasionally.

- Meanwhile, in a mixing bowl, combine egg yolks, remaining ⅓ cup sugar, and cornstarch, whisking until smooth.
- When puree mixture comes to a boil, gradually add a little to egg mixture to temper, whisking constantly to prevent eggs from curdling. Add tempered egg mixture to puree mixture in saucepan, whisking well. Cook over medium-high heat, whisking constantly. When curd begins to stiffen, alternate using a rubber spatula and a wire whisk to ensure mixture does not burn on bottom of pan. Once curd comes to a boil, remove from heat, and pour into a shallow pan.
- Cover surface of curd with plastic wrap to prevent a skin from forming. Refrigerate until cold, 4 to 6 hours, before using.

If frozen cherry puree is not available, in a saucepan, combine 1 (16-ounce) package frozen pitted cherries and ¼ cup sugar. Cook over medium heat until sugar dissolves. Let cool slightly before transferring mixture to the work bowl of a food processor. Process until smooth.

White Chocolate–Jasmine Tea Fudge
(photo on page 118)
Gluten-free | *Yield: approximately 48 pieces*

7 tea bags Jasmine green tea, divided
5 tablespoons boiling water
1 cup unsalted butter
4 cups granulated sugar
⅓ cup sour cream
1 teaspoon salt
2 (12-ounce) packages white chocolate morsels
2 (7-ounce) jars marshmallow crème
2 teaspoons vanilla extract
Garnish: 1 recipe Wet Walnuts (recipe follows)

- Line a 13x9-inch baking pan with parchment paper, letting paper hang over sides. Coat parchment paper with butter.
- Using scissors, cut open 6 tea bags, and place dried tea leaves in a heatproof measuring cup. Pour boiling water over tea leaves. Let steep for 5 to 10 minutes. Strain tea, pressing out and reserving infused liquid and discarding leaves.
- In a large saucepan, melt butter over medium-high heat. Add sugar, sour cream, salt, and reserved tea liquid, stirring well. Cook at low heat until sugar dissolves, stirring constantly. Increase heat to medium, and cook until a candy thermometer registers 235°.
- Remove from heat, and add white chocolate, marshmallow crème, and vanilla extract, stirring until well blended. (If necessary, return pan to stove briefly to melt chocolate.) Spread fudge into prepared pan.

- Before fudge sets, cut open remaining 1 tea bag, and sprinkle tea leaves over fudge.
- Let cool for 4 to 6 hours.
- Using parchment paper overhang, lift fudge from pan, and place on a cutting board. Cut fudge into 1½-inch squares.
- Garnish each fudge square with a Wet Walnut just before serving, if desired.

Wet Walnuts
Gluten-free | *Yield: 2 cups*

1 cup sugar
1 cup boiling water
1½ cups walnut halves

- In a heatproof bowl, combine sugar and boiling water, stirring until sugar dissolves. Let simple syrup cool slightly.
- Add walnuts to syrup, stirring to coat. Cover, and refrigerate for 3 to 4 days before using.

WINDSOR COURT HOTEL
english-style tea in the crescent city

Afternoon tea at Le Salon in Windsor Court's elegantly appointed lobby has been a fixture in New Orleans since the hotel opened 32 years ago.

Windsor Court Hotel
300 Gravier Street
New Orleans, LA 70130
504-523-6000
windsorcourthotel.com

Establishing a new tradition in a place as old as New Orleans, the Louisiana city that has straddled the Mississippi River for almost three centuries, is not an easy accomplishment. But in just over three decades, afternoon tea at Le Salon, the elegantly appointed lobby of the Windsor Court, has been embraced by generations of people in the Crescent City.

Across Canal Street from the French Quarter in the city's Central Business District, the Windsor Court opened its doors in 1984. "We've offered afternoon tea almost since day one," says Jennifer Gunning, Food and Beverage Manager of Le Salon's tearoom. "It was an instant hit." Since then, Le Salon's tea service has only grown in popularity. "We were one of the first places in New Orleans to offer afternoon tea, and we are still one of the few places that do."

Along the way, New Orleans has embraced afternoon tea as a way to celebrate everything from baby showers to college graduations. "That's one of the things I love about what I do," Jennifer says. "As a kid, I used to love having tea parties with my stuffed animals. Now I get to have tea parties for baby showers, debutante parties, and bridal showers."

Le Salon's afternoon tea is a traditional English tea service, complete with two types of scones (black currant and walnut) served with raspberry preserves, Devonshire cream, and lemon curd and 26 varieties of loose-leaf tea—from white teas to blended blacks. The tea sandwiches include traditional but clever combinations—from a classic cucumber with a dill spread on rye bread to a curried chicken salad with just the right amount of spice. Shun Li, the hotel's pastry chef, creates extravagant desserts for the sweets course, among them, house-made almond cakes and a variety of truffles, small chocolates, and miniature tartlets. The flavors change seasonally.

Tea is offered Thursday through Sunday year-around, but the Windsor Court steps things up a notch during the holiday season with its holiday teas. A 20-foot Christmas tree transforms the lobby into a winter wonderland, and a profusion of poinsettias fill Le Salon's planter boxes. Beginning after Thanksgiving, Le Salon offers afternoon tea more frequently, and by the week of Christmas, there are multiple seatings every day.

Partaking in the Windsor Court's Holiday Tea has become a tradition for many local families. When reservations open each year on March 1, patrons begin calling to reserve their favorite table. (The table in front of the fireplace is a highly coveted spot.) "By the middle of April or the first of May, a lot of our days are fully booked," Jennifer points out. "People have standing reservations year after year for their families.

"We have one group of ladies who have been coming here for holiday tea since they were in college," Jennifer continues. Originally sorority sisters, now they bring their children and grandchildren. "What was once a party of five is now a party of 25," she notes.

After all, afternoon tea at the Windsor Court is a long-standing New Orleans tradition.

Traditional English-style afternoon tea at the Windsor Court is served on Wedgwood's classic Wild Strawberry pattern. Above left, the table before the fireplace is one of the most sought-after reservations for tea during the holidays.

Courtesy of Windsor Court Hotel

- Add mayonnaise and white pepper to chives mixture, whisking to blend. Add lobster meat, tossing gently to coat. Refrigerate until cold, if desired, or use immediately.
- Just before serving, place 1 tablespoon lobster salad on each cucumber slice.
- Garnish each with shredded mango, if desired.

If live lobsters are not available, substitute 5 medium lobster tails. Cook in boiling salted water until meat is white and opaque, 2 to 3 minutes.

Curried Chicken Salad Canapés
Yield: 48

1½ pounds boneless skinless chicken breasts
1 tablespoon olive oil
½ teaspoon salt
¼ teaspoon ground white pepper
½ cup mayonnaise
2 to 5 teaspoons curry powder, according to taste
1 tablespoon fresh lime juice
¼ cup chopped celery
½ teaspoon minced shallot
12 slices white country-style bread
Garnish: roasted red pepper strips, fresh cilantro

- Preheat oven to 350°.
- Line a rimmed baking sheet with aluminum foil.
- Season chicken with olive oil, salt, and pepper. Place on prepared baking sheet.
- Roast until an instant-read thermometer registers 165° when inserted in the thickest part of chicken breasts, approximately 15 minutes.
- Transfer chicken to a plate, and let cool for 10 minutes. Chop into very small pieces.
- In a large bowl, combine mayonnaise, curry powder, and lime juice, whisking to blend. Add cooled chicken, celery, and shallot, stirring gently. Taste, and adjust seasoning if necessary.
- Using a 2¼-inch round cutter, cut 48 shapes from bread slices*. Divide chicken salad among bread rounds.
- Garnish each canapé with roasted red pepper strips and cilantro, if desired.

If bread is very soft, freeze bread before cutting.

Lobster Salad on Cucumber Rounds
Gluten-free | *Yield: approximately 26*

2 tablespoons fresh lemon juice
1 tablespoon finely chopped fresh chives
½ teaspoon salt
2 (1.5-pound) live lobsters*
¼ cup mayonnaise
¼ teaspoon ground white pepper
1 English cucumber, cut into ¼-inch slices
Garnish: coarsely grated ripe mango

- In a large bowl, combine lemon juice, chives, and salt. Let stand at room temperature for 30 minutes.
- Meanwhile, in an 8-quart stockpot of boiling salted water, plunge lobsters headfirst. Loosely cover pot, and cook lobsters over medium-high heat for 6 minutes. Remove lobsters from pot, and let cool.
- When lobsters are cool, remove meat from claws, joints, and tails, and finely chop.

Currant Scones
Yield: 18

3¾ cups plus 2 tablespoons all-purpose flour
¼ cup plus 3 tablespoons sugar, divided
¾ teaspoon baking powder
⅝ teaspoon baking soda
¼ teaspoon salt
7½ tablespoons cold unsalted butter, cut into pieces
1½ cups (6 ounces) dried currants
1¼ cups plus 2 tablespoons whole buttermilk
1 tablespoon heavy whipping cream

• Preheat oven to 350°.
• Line 2 rimmed baking sheets with parchment paper.
• In a large bowl, combine flour, ¼ cup plus 1 table-spoon sugar, baking powder, baking soda, and salt, whisking well. Using a pastry blender, cut butter into flour mixture until it resembles coarse crumbs. Add currants, stirring to combine.
• Add buttermilk, stirring until mixture is evenly moist. (If dough seems dry, add more buttermilk, 1 tablespoon at a time.) Working gently, bring mixture together with hands until a dough forms.
• On a lightly floured surface, roll out dough to a 1-inch thickness. Using a 2¼-inch round cutter, cut 18 scones from dough, rerolling scraps as necessary. Place scones 2 inches apart on prepared baking sheets.
• Brush tops of scones with cream, and sprinkle with remaining 2 tablespoons sugar.
• Bake until scones are lightly golden, 15 to 20 minutes.

Windsor Court Madeleines
Yield: approximately 72

5 large eggs
2 cups sugar
4 teaspoons cream of tartar
4 cups cake flour
4 teaspoons baking powder
1 teaspoon salt
1 cup whole milk
1 vanilla bean, split and seeds scraped and reserved
1 teaspoon fresh lemon zest*
1 cup unsalted butter, melted
Garnish: melted white chocolate or dark chocolate

• Preheat oven to 350°.
• Lightly spray several 12-well large madeleine pans with baking spray with flour.

• In a large bowl, combine eggs, sugar, and cream of tartar. Beat at high speed with a mixer until batter reaches the ribbon stage, 5 to 8 minutes. (When beater is lifted, batter will fall slowly back into batter in ribbon-like strands.)
• In a separate bowl, combine flour, baking powder, and salt, whisking well. Add flour mixture to egg mixture, folding gently to combine. (Be careful not to overwork batter.)
• In a liquid-measuring cup, combine milk, reserved vanilla bean seeds, and lemon zest, stirring to blend. Add milk mixture and melted butter to batter, folding gently to blend.
• Spoon batter into prepared madeleine pans, filling wells no more than halfway.
• Bake in batches until madeleines are golden brown, approximately 15 minutes. Remove from pans, and let cool completely on wire racks.
• Garnish madeleines by dipping into melted choco-late, if desired. Let set before serving.

For featherlight strands of lemon zest, grate lemon peel with a Microplane grater.

Tea-Steeping *Guide*

The quality of the tea served at afternoon tea is as important as the food and the décor. To be sure your infusion is successful every time, here are some basic guidelines to follow.

WATER

Always use the best water possible. If the water tastes good, so will your tea. Heat the water on the stove top or in an electric kettle to the desired temperature. A microwave oven is not recommended.

TEMPERATURE

Heating the water to the correct temperature is arguably one of the most important factors in making a great pot of tea. Pouring boiling water on green, white, or oolong tea leaves can result in a very unpleasant brew. Always refer to the tea purveyor's packaging for specific instructions, but in general, use 170° to 195° water for these delicate tea types. Reserve boiling (212°) water for black and puerh teas, as well as herbal and fruit tisanes.

TEAPOT

If the teapot you plan to use is delicate, warm it with hot tap water first to avert possible cracking. Discard this water before adding the tea leaves or tea bags.

TEA

Use the highest-quality tea you can afford, whether loose leaf or prepackaged in bags or sachets. Remember that these better teas can often be steeped more than once. When using loose-leaf tea, generally use 1 generous teaspoon of dry leaf per 8 ounces of water, and use an infuser basket. For a stronger infusion, add another teaspoonful or two of dry tea leaf.

TIME

As soon as the water reaches the correct temperature for the type of tea, pour it over the leaves or tea bag in the teapot, and cover the pot with a lid. Set a timer—usually 1 to 2 minutes for whites and oolongs; 2 to 3 minutes for greens; and 3 to 5 minutes for blacks, puerhs, and herbals. (Steeping tea longer than recommended can yield a bitter infusion.) When the timer goes off, remove the infuser basket or the tea bags from the teapot.

ENJOYMENT

For best flavor, serve the tea as soon as possible. Keep the beverage warm atop a lighted warmer or under your favorite tea cozy if necessary.

Chocolate-
Raspberry Bars
page 114

Acknowledgments

Credits

PHOTOGRAPHY
Bruce Richardson: 85–88, 97–98, 100, 106
Jim Bathie: 11, 13–14, 31, 34–36, 123–124, 126–127
John O'Hagan: cover, 1, 5, 9–10, 12, 23–30, 43–48, 49–54, 58–62, 69–74, 77–84, 88–90, 91–96, 129, back cover
Lana Farfan: 55–58
Melissa and Jeff Placzek: 7, 37–42
Queen Mary Tea Room: 80
Sarah Arrington: 63–68
The St. James Tearoom: 99–102
Stephanie Welbourne: 3–4, 15–22, 114, 131, 135
Taj Boston: 103–108
Willard InterContinental: 115–120
William Dickey: 109–113
Windsor Court Hotel: 121, 124–125, 128

TEXT
Betty Terry: 24–25, 44–45, 78–79, 86–87, 122–123
Bruce Richardson: 70–71, 98–99
Janece Maze: 16–17, 50–51, 64–65, 92–93, 104–105, 116–117
Lorna Reeves: 10–11, 32–33, 38–39, 56–57, 110–111

Resources

TITLE PAGE
Page 1: Royal Crown Derby *Derby Posies* salad plate, cup, and saucer.*

TABLE OF CONTENTS
Page 5: Royal Albert *Lady Carlyle* salad plate; Royal Albert *Moss Rose* cup and saucer.* Silver-plated teapot from Tea for Two, 888-601-9990, *teafortwo.com.*

INTRODUCTION
Page 7: Royal Albert *Old Country Roses* dinner plate, salad plate, cup, and saucer.*

CAMELLIA'S SIN TEA PARLOR
Page 11: Royal Albert *Moss Rose* cream soup bowl; Towle *King Richard* cream soup spoon.*
Page 13: Demitasse spoon set with teapot handle from Tea for Two, 888-601-9990, *teafortwo.com.*

HEIRLOOMS TEA ROOM
Page 37: Royal Albert *Old Country Roses* dinner plate, salad plate, cup, and saucer.*
Page 40: Royal Albert *Old Country Roses* dinner plate, cup, saucer, teapot, creamer, and sugar bowl.*

LADY BEDFORD'S TEA PARLOUR
Page 43: Noritake *Mimi* salad plate, sugar bowl, cup, and saucer.*
Pages 45, 47–48: Noritake *Mimi* salad plate, cup, and saucer.* *Sunny Day* wrap around tea cozy from Thistle Down Cozies, 877-890-9106, *thistledowncozies.com.*

PARIS IN A CUP
Page 58: *PersonaliTEA* black teapot from Adagio, *adagio.com.*
Page 60: Towle *King Richard* teaspoon.*
Page 61: White Pedestal Medium from Rosanna, 877-343-3779, *rosannainc.com. PersonaliTEA* teapot from Adagio, *adagio.com.*

QUEEN MARY TEA ROOM
Page 82: Royal Albert *Lady Carlyle* salad plate; Royal Albert *Moss Rose* cup and saucer.* Silver-plated teapot from Tea for Two, 888-601-9990, *teafortwo.com.*

ROSE TREE COTTAGE
Pages 89–90: Royal Crown Derby *Derby Posies* cup and saucer and salad plate* Demitasse spoon set with teapot handle from Tea for Two, 888-601-9990, *teafortwo.com.*

TAJ BOSTON
Pages 103, 106, 108: Wedgwood *Butterfly Bloom* teapot, 2-tier cake stand, tea plate set, cups, and saucers from Macy's, *www1.macys.com.*

TEABERRY'S TEA ROOM
Page 113: Royal Albert *Lady Carlyle* salad plate, cup, and saucer.*

THE WINDSOR COURT HOTEL
Pages 123–128: Wedgwood *Wild Strawberry* teapot, cream pitcher, sugar bowl, cup, saucer, and salad plate.*

TEA-STEEPING GUIDE
Page 129: *Margaret* cup and saucer from Porcelain Treasures, 888-832-5005, *porcelaintreasures.com.*

ACKNOWLEDGMENTS
Page 131: Royal Albert *Lady Carlyle* salad plate, cup, and saucer.*

RECIPE INDEX
Page 133: Noritake *Mimi* salad plate, cream pitcher, and sugar bowl.* *Sunny Day* wrap around tea cozy from Thistle Down Cozies, 877-890-9106, *thistledowncozies.com.*
Page 135: Royal Crown Derby *Derby Posies* dinner plate, salad plate, cup, and saucer.*

*from Replacements, Ltd., 800-REPLACE, replacements.com.

Editor's Note: *Items not listed are from private collections. No pattern or manufacturer information was available at press time.*

Cream Puffs
page 48

Recipe Index

Editor's Note: *Recipes listed in coral are gluten-free, provided gluten-free versions of processed ingredients (such as condiments, precooked meat, stocks, and wraps) are used.*

"Tearooms offer us the opportunity to step out of the ordinary and into the extraordinary for a few hours."

—SHARON GILLEY, *owner of The English Rose Tea Room in Chattanooga, Tennessee*